AIR FRYER RECIPE INSTRUCTOR

THE ART AND SCIENCE OF AIR FRYING

ALBERT RAMSEY

Copyright © 2024 ALBERT RAMSEY

All rights reserved. No part of this publication may be reproduced, distributed, or transmitted in any form or by any means, including photocopying, recording, or other electronic or mechanical methods, without the prior written permission of the publisher, except in the case of brief quotations embodied in critical reviews and certain other noncommercial uses permitted by copyright law.

Table of Contents

Introduction 16
Chapter 1 19
Crispy Classic Chicken Wings 19
Chapter 2 23
Golden French Fries Mastery 23
Chapter 3 27
Perfectly Grilled Salmon 27
Chapter 4 31
Zesty Lemon Herb Chicken 31
Chapter 5 35
Vegetarian Spring Rolls 35
Chapter 6 39
Savory Garlic Parmesan Brussels Sprouts 39
Chapter 7: 43
Homemade Crispy Onion Rings 43
Chapter 8 47
Spicy Sweet Potato Fries 47
Chapter 9 51
Air-Fried BBQ Chicken Drumsticks 51

Chapter 10 55
Crispy Coconut Shrimp 55
Chapter 11 59
Mouthwatering Teriyaki Salmon 59
Chapter 12 63
Stuffed Portobello Mushrooms 63
Chapter 13 67
Air-Fried Falafel with Tahini Sauce 67
Chapter 14 72
Cajun Spiced Sweet Potato Chips 72
Chapter 15 76
Lemon Garlic Parmesan Asparagus 76
Chapter 16 80
Crispy Coconut Chicken Tenders 80
Chapter 17 84
Mango Salsa Stuffed Avocado 84
Chapter 18 88
Garlic Herb Roasted Potatoes 88
Chapter 19 92
Buffalo Cauliflower Bites 92

Chapter 20 97
Chocolate Lava Cake Surprise 97
Chapter 21 101
Caprese Stuffed Portobello Mushrooms 101
Chapter 22 103
Cinnamon Sugar Apple Chips 103
Chapter 23 104
Pesto Shrimp Skewers 104
Chapter 24 105
Mediterranean Stuffed Bell Peppers 105
Chapter 25 107
Teriyaki Pineapple Chicken Skewers 107
Chapter 26 109
Southwest Stuffed Sweet Potatoes 109
Chapter 27 110
Lemon Herb Quinoa Cakes 110
Chapter 28 112
Balsamic Glazed Brussels Sprouts 112
Chapter 29 114
Panko-Crusted Zucchini Fries 114

Chapter 30 115
Maple Glazed Salmon with Roasted Vegetables
.... 115
Chapter 31 117
Avocado Egg Rolls with Sriracha Dipping Sauce
.... 117
Chapter 32 118
Greek-Style Stuffed Peppers 118
Chapter 33 120
Orange Glazed Chicken Drumsticks 120
Chapter 34 121
Spinach and Feta Stuffed Chicken Breast 121
Chapter 35 123
Maple Bacon Wrapped Shrimp 123
Chapter 36 124
Teriyaki Tofu Stir-Fry 124
Chapter 37 126
Tex-Mex Loaded Sweet Potato Skins 126
Chapter 38 128
Hawaiian Chicken Kabobs 128

Chapter 39 129
Lemon Blueberry Muffins............................... 129
Chapter 40 131
Cajun Shrimp Tacos 131
Chapter 41 132
Crispy Zucchini Parmesan Chips.................... 132
Chapter 42 134
Mediterranean Quinoa Salad with Lemon Vinaigrette 134
Chapter 43 135
Spiced Butternut Squash Fries 135
Chapter 44 137
Garlic Butter Shrimp Pasta 137
Chapter 45 138
Caramelized Banana Sundaes 138
Chapter 46 140
Pesto Zoodles with Cherry Tomatoes.............. 140
Chapter 47 141
Raspberry Balsamic Glazed Chicken 141
Chapter 48 143

Buffalo Cauliflower Tacos 143

Chapter 49 144

Caprese Stuffed Chicken Breast 144

Chapter 50 146

Apple Cinnamon Oatmeal Cookies.................. 146

Chapter 51 147

Mediterranean Stuffed Bell Peppers................ 147

Chapter 52 149

Spinach and Mushroom Quesadillas 149

Chapter 53 150

Teriyaki Pineapple Chicken Skewers............... 150

Chapter 54 152

Lemon Dill Roasted Brussels Sprouts 152

Chapter 55 153

Chocolate Covered Strawberry Empanadas.... 153

Chapter 56 155

Crispy Parmesan Zucchini Fries...................... 155

Chapter 57 156

Thai Basil Chicken Lettuce Wraps................... 156

Chapter 58 158

Caprese Air-Fried Avocado 158

Chapter 59 159

Lemon Blueberry Pancake Bites 159

Chapter 60 160

BBQ Pulled Pork Stuffed Sweet Potatoes 160

Chapter 61 162

Teriyaki Vegetable Stir-Fry 162

Chapter 62 163

Blackened Salmon Tacos 163

Chapter 63 165

Mediterranean Eggplant Slices 165

Chapter 64 166

Pesto Mozzarella Stuffed Mushrooms 166

Chapter 65 168

Cinnamon Sugar Apple Chips 168

Chapter 66 169

Caprese Stuffed Mushrooms 169

Chapter 67 170

Garlic Rosemary Hasselback Potatoes 170

Chapter 68 172

Coconut Lime Shrimp Skewers 172

Chapter 69 173

Maple Dijon Glazed Brussels Sprouts 173

Chapter 70 174

Lemon Garlic Shrimp Pasta 174

Chapter 71 176

Balsamic Glazed Portobello Mushrooms 176

Chapter 72 177

Panko Crusted Chicken Tenders 177

Chapter 73 179

Chili Lime Corn on the Cob 179

Chapter 74 180

Southwest Stuffed Bell Peppers 180

Chapter 75 182

Spinach and Feta Stuffed Chicken Breasts 182

Chapter 76 183

Lemon Herb Quinoa Salad 183

Chapter 77 185

Honey Sriracha Glazed Chicken Wings 185

Chapter 78 186

Blueberry Balsamic Glazed Salmon 186

Chapter 79 188

Cajun Shrimp and Sausage Skewers 188

Chapter 81 189

Spinach and Artichoke Stuffed Chicken........... 189

Chapter 82 191

Sweet and Spicy Pineapple Shrimp Skewers .. 191

Chapter 83 192

Coconut Lime Chicken Tenders 192

Chapter 84 194

Herb-Marinated Lamb Chops 194

Chapter 85 195

Raspberry Almond Mini Cheesecakes............. 195

Chapter 86 197

BBQ Pulled Chicken Sliders 197

Chapter 87 198

Lemon Poppy Seed Donuts............................. 198

Chapter 88 200

Buffalo Chicken Meatballs 200

Chapter 89 201

Cilantro Lime Shrimp Tacos 201
Chapter 90 203
Chocolate Peanut Butter Banana Empanadas 203
Chapter 91 204
Greek Chicken Souvlaki Skewers..................... 204
Chapter 92 206
Raspberry Chocolate Chip Pancakes 206
Chapter 93 207
Garlic Butter Steak Bites 207
PHASE II 209
Introduction to Air Frying 210
Brief History and Evolution of Air Frying Technology.. 210
Overview of the Benefits of Air Frying Compared to Traditional Cooking Methods 211
Chapter 1 213
Choosing the Right Air Fryer 213
Types of Air Fryers Available in the Market 213
Factors to Consider When Selecting the Best Air Fryer for Your Needs 215
Chapter 2 218

Understanding How Air Fryers Work**............218

The Science Behind Air Frying and Its Cooking Mechanism..218

Explaining Convection and Rapid Air Technology 220

Chapter 3 222

Essential Tools and Accessories......................222

Must-Have Tools and Accessories for Efficient Air Frying 222

Tips on Maintaining and Cleaning Your Air Fryer 224

Chapter 4 226

Mastering Air Fryer Controls............................226

A Detailed Guide to the Various Settings and Controls on an Air Fryer 227

Troubleshooting Common Issues with Air Fryer Operation 229

Chapter 5 231

Prepping Ingredients for Air Frying 231

Properly Preparing Ingredients for Optimal Air Frying Results 231

Tips on Marinating and Seasoning for Enhanced Flavors 233

Chapter 6 236

Appetizers and Snacks 236

A Collection of Delicious and Crispy Appetizers and Snacks 236

Creative Ideas for Unique Air-Fried Starters 238

Chapter 7 241

Healthy Air Fryer Cooking 241

Strategies for Creating Healthier Versions of Your Favorite Fried Foods 241

Nutritional Benefits of Air Frying 243

Chapter 8 246

Main Course Mastery 246

Recipes for Succulent Air-Fried Meats, Poultry, and Seafood 246

Techniques for Achieving the Perfect Balance of Crispiness and Juiciness 248

Chapter 9 251

Vegetarian Delights 251

Mouthwatering Air-Fried Vegetarian and Vegan Dishes 251

Tips for Preserving the Natural Flavors and Textures of Vegetables 253

Chapter 10 256

Sweets and Treats 256

Delectable Desserts and Sweet Treats Made in the Air Fryer 256

Exploring the Versatility of the Air Fryer Beyond Savory Dishes 258

INTRODUCTION

Welcome to the world of culinary innovation and convenience! In "Air Fryer Recipe Instructor: The Art and Science of Air Frying," we embark on a culinary journey that transcends traditional cooking methods, unlocking the full potential of one of the most revolutionary kitchen appliances—the air fryer. As we delve into the art and science of air frying, you'll discover a myriad of techniques, tips, and tantalizing recipes that promise to transform your cooking experience.

The air fryer, with its remarkable ability to crisp and cook with minimal oil, has taken the cooking landscape by storm. This book serves as your comprehensive guide, designed not only to teach you the fundamentals of air frying but to elevate your culinary skills to new heights. Whether you're a novice in the kitchen or a seasoned chef, the recipes and insights within these pages cater to all levels of expertise.

In the following chapters, we'll explore a diverse array of dishes—from classic favorites to contemporary creations—each meticulously crafted to showcase the versatility and efficiency of the air fryer. From perfectly crispy chicken wings to mouthwatering chocolate lava cakes, you'll witness the transformation of ordinary ingredients into extraordinary meals.

But this book goes beyond just recipes. It's a holistic exploration of the science behind air frying, unraveling the mysteries of temperature, timing, and technique. Understanding the artistry of flavor infusion and texture mastery, you'll gain the confidence to experiment with your own culinary creations, adapting and innovating as you see fit.

So, whether you're looking to create healthier versions of your favorite fried foods or eager to expand your culinary repertoire, "Air Fryer Recipe Instructor" is your trusted companion. Let the aroma of sizzling spices and the sound of perfectly crisped delicacies entice you as we embark on a delicious adventure, where the art and science of air frying converge to redefine the way you experience and enjoy food. Get ready to revolutionize your kitchen and become a maestro of the air fryer!

CHAPTER 1

CRISPY CLASSIC CHICKEN WINGS

Welcome to the delicious world of air frying, where we begin our journey with a classic favorite—the Crispy Classic Chicken Wings. In this chapter, we'll delve into the fundamentals of achieving perfection: crispy, flavorful chicken wings that are bound to become a staple in your culinary repertoire.

Ingredients:

- 2 pounds of chicken wings, split at joints, tips discarded
- 2 tablespoons of baking powder
- 1 teaspoon of salt
- 1 teaspoon of garlic powder
- 1 teaspoon of onion powder
- 1/2 teaspoon of smoked paprika
- 1/2 teaspoon of black pepper

Air Fryer Machine Settings:

- Preheat your air fryer to 400°F (200°C). Preheating ensures that the chicken wings start cooking immediately, contributing to that coveted crispiness.

Time:

- Cook the wings for 24-26 minutes, flipping halfway through. The precise timing ensures an even cook, rendering the wings crispy on the outside and juicy on the inside.

Method:

1. Prepare the Chicken Wings:
- Pat the chicken wings dry with paper towels. Dry wings are crucial for achieving crispiness in the air fryer.

2. Season the Wings:

- In a large bowl, toss the wings with baking powder, salt, garlic powder, onion powder, smoked paprika, and black pepper. The baking powder is the secret ingredient that contributes to the wings' crispiness.

3. Preheat the Air Fryer:
- Preheat your air fryer to 400°F (200°C) for about 3-5 minutes. This step is essential for jumpstarting the cooking process and ensuring that the wings cook evenly.

4. Air Fry the Wings:
- Place the seasoned wings in a single layer in the air fryer basket, ensuring they are not overcrowded. Cook for 12-13 minutes, flip the wings, and cook for an additional 12-13 minutes until golden brown and crispy.

5. Check for Doneness:

- To ensure the wings are cooked thoroughly, check for an internal temperature of 165°F (74°C). The air fryer's high heat achieves the perfect balance between crispiness and succulence.

Serving:

- Serve these Crispy Classic Chicken Wings hot, accompanied by your favorite dipping sauces—whether it's a classic buffalo sauce, tangy blue cheese dressing, or a zesty ranch dip. These wings are perfect for game nights, gatherings, or as a satisfying treat for yourself.

Now that you've mastered the art and science of creating crispy chicken wings with your air fryer, get ready to explore more culinary delights in the chapters that follow. Happy air frying!

CHAPTER 2

GOLDEN FRENCH FRIES MASTERY

In this chapter, we embark on a culinary adventure to master the art of creating the perfect Golden French Fries using your trusty air fryer. Get ready to indulge in the crispiness and golden perfection that will rival any traditional deep-fried version. We'll explore the science behind achieving that ideal balance between a crunchy exterior and a fluffy interior.

Ingredients:

- 4 large russet potatoes, peeled and cut into uniform matchsticks
6. 2 tablespoons of vegetable oil
7. 1 teaspoon of garlic powder
8. 1 teaspoon of paprika
9. Salt, to taste
10. Freshly ground black pepper, to taste

Air Fryer Machine Settings:

- Preheat your air fryer to 400°F (200°C). Preheating ensures a quick and even cooking process, resulting in those coveted golden fries.

Time:

- Cook the fries for 18-22 minutes, shaking or stirring halfway through. This ensures all sides of the fries get that perfect crispiness.

Method:

1. Prepare the Potatoes:
- Peel and cut the potatoes into uniform matchsticks. Soak them in cold water for 30 minutes to remove excess starch, then thoroughly pat them dry.

2. Season the Fries:
- In a large bowl, toss the dried fries with vegetable oil, garlic powder, paprika, salt, and

freshly ground black pepper. Ensure the fries are evenly coated with the seasoning.

3. Preheat the Air Fryer:
- Preheat your air fryer to 400°F (200°C) for about 3-5 minutes. Preheating is crucial for achieving that immediate crisping effect.

4. Air Fry the Fries:
- Place the seasoned fries in a single layer in the air fryer basket. Cook for 9-11 minutes, shake or stir the fries to ensure even cooking, and continue to cook for an additional 9-11 minutes or until golden brown and crispy.

5. Check for Doneness:
- To ensure the fries are perfectly cooked, taste-test a few for that ideal combination of a crispy exterior and a fluffy interior.

Serving:

- Serve these Golden French Fries hot and crispy, perhaps with a sprinkle of additional salt if desired. Accompany them with an array of dipping sauces—classic ketchup, tangy mayonnaise, or a homemade aioli. The beauty of these fries lies not just in their texture but in their versatility, making them an ideal side for any meal.

Congratulations on mastering the art and science of creating Golden French Fries in your air fryer. Get ready to explore more culinary delights in the upcoming chapters of "Air Fryer Recipe Instructor." Happy air frying!

CHAPTER 3
PERFECTLY GRILLED SALMON

Dive into the world of seafood perfection as we explore the delicate balance of achieving a perfectly grilled salmon using your air fryer. In this chapter, we'll unravel the secrets to creating a delightful dish where the skin is crispy, and the inside is tender and moist—a true testament to the art and science of air frying.

Ingredients:

- 4 salmon fillets, skin-on
- 2 tablespoons olive oil
- 1 teaspoon lemon zest
- 1 teaspoon dried dill
- 1 teaspoon garlic powder
- Salt and pepper, to taste
- Lemon wedges, for serving

Air Fryer Machine Settings:

- Preheat your air fryer to 400°F (200°C). Preheating ensures that the salmon starts cooking immediately, allowing for that perfect sear on the skin.

Time:

- Cook the salmon for 10-12 minutes, depending on thickness, flipping halfway through. This method ensures a crispy skin while maintaining the moistness of the salmon.

Method:

1. Prepare the Salmon:
- Pat the salmon fillets dry with paper towels. This step is essential to ensure the skin crisps up during the air-frying process.

2. Season the Salmon:

- In a small bowl, mix together olive oil, lemon zest, dried dill, garlic powder, salt, and pepper. Brush the mixture over the salmon fillets, ensuring even coverage.

3. Preheat the Air Fryer:
- Preheat your air fryer to 400°F (200°C) for about 3-5 minutes. Preheating sets the stage for achieving that ideal crispiness on the salmon skin.

4. Air Fry the Salmon:
- Place the seasoned salmon fillets in the air fryer basket, skin side down. Cook for 5-6 minutes, flip the fillets, and continue to cook for an additional 5-6 minutes or until the salmon reaches your desired level of doneness.

5. Check for Doneness:
- To ensure the salmon is perfectly cooked, use a fork to gently flake the fish. The flesh should be

opaque and easily separated, while the skin should be crispy.

Serving:

- Serve the Perfectly Grilled Salmon hot, garnished with fresh dill and accompanied by lemon wedges. Consider pairing it with a light salad, quinoa, or roasted vegetables for a well-rounded meal. The combination of crispy skin and moist, flavorful salmon makes this dish a true sensation for your taste buds.

Congratulations on mastering the art and science of air-frying salmon. Get ready to explore more culinary wonders in the upcoming chapters of "Air Fryer Recipe Instructor." Happy air frying!

CHAPTER 4
ZESTY LEMON HERB CHICKEN

In this chapter, we embark on a culinary journey to discover the perfect harmony of flavors in our Zesty Lemon Herb Chicken, showcasing the remarkable ability of the air fryer to infuse every bite with a burst of citrusy zest and aromatic herbs while retaining the chicken's natural moisture. Get ready to elevate your taste experience with this delightful and flavorful recipe.

Ingredients:

- 4 boneless, skinless chicken breasts
- 3 tablespoons olive oil
- Zest of 1 lemon
- Juice of 1 lemon
- 2 teaspoons dried oregano
- 2 teaspoons dried thyme
- 1 teaspoon garlic powder

- Salt and pepper, to taste
- Fresh parsley, chopped, for garnish

Air Fryer Machine Settings:

- Preheat your air fryer to 375°F (190°C). Preheating ensures that the chicken starts cooking immediately, sealing in the flavors and moisture.

Time:

- Cook the chicken for 18-20 minutes, flipping halfway through. This method allows for even cooking and the development of a golden, flavorful crust.

Method:

1. Prepare the Chicken:
- Pat the chicken breasts dry with paper towels. This step ensures a good sear and helps the seasoning adhere to the chicken.

2. Season the Chicken:
   - In a bowl, mix together olive oil, lemon zest, lemon juice, dried oregano, dried thyme, garlic powder, salt, and pepper. Coat the chicken breasts evenly with the mixture.

3. Preheat the Air Fryer:
   - Preheat your air fryer to 375°F (190°C) for about 3-5 minutes. Preheating sets the stage for achieving that perfect balance of tenderness and flavor infusion.

4. Air Fry the Chicken:
   - Place the seasoned chicken breasts in the air fryer basket. Cook for 9-10 minutes, flip the breasts, and continue to cook for an additional 9-10 minutes or until the internal temperature reaches 165°F (74°C).

5. Check for Doneness:

- Use a meat thermometer to ensure the chicken is cooked through. The juices should run clear, and the center should no longer be pink.

Serving:

- Serve the Zesty Lemon Herb Chicken hot, garnished with fresh parsley. Pair it with your favorite sides—roasted vegetables, rice, or a light salad. The vibrant flavors and juicy tenderness of the chicken make this dish a standout option for any occasion.

Congratulations on exploring the flavorful world of Zesty Lemon Herb Chicken with your air fryer. Get ready to dive into more culinary delights in the upcoming chapters of "Air Fryer Recipe Instructor." Happy air frying!

CHAPTER 5

VEGETARIAN SPRING ROLLS

Embark on a journey into the vibrant world of vegetarian cuisine as we explore the creation of Crispy and Healthy Vegetarian Spring Rolls using your air fryer. This chapter celebrates the art and science of crafting delicate spring rolls filled with an array of colorful vegetables, promising a delightful combination of crunch and nutrition in every bite.

Ingredients:

For the Filling:

- 2 cups shredded cabbage
- 1 cup julienned carrots
- 1 cup bean sprouts
- 1 cup thinly sliced bell peppers (assorted colors)
- 1 cup sliced shiitake mushrooms
- 3 green onions, thinly sliced
- 2 tablespoons soy sauce

- 1 tablespoon sesame oil
- 1 teaspoon grated ginger
- 1 teaspoon garlic powder
- Salt and pepper, to taste

For the Spring Rolls:

- 12 spring roll wrappers
- 2 tablespoons cornstarch mixed with 2 tablespoons water (for sealing)

Air Fryer Machine Settings:

- Preheat your air fryer to 375°F (190°C). Preheating ensures a quick and even cooking process, resulting in golden and crispy spring rolls.

Time:

- Cook the spring rolls for 10-12 minutes, turning halfway through. This method ensures that all sides achieve the desired crispiness.

Method:

1. Prepare the Filling:
   - In a large bowl, combine shredded cabbage, julienned carrots, bean sprouts, sliced bell peppers, shiitake mushrooms, and green onions. Toss with soy sauce, sesame oil, grated ginger, garlic powder, salt, and pepper.

2. Prepare the Spring Rolls:
   - Lay a spring roll wrapper on a clean surface. Spoon 2-3 tablespoons of the vegetable filling onto the wrapper. Fold the sides inward and roll tightly, sealing the edges with the cornstarch-water mixture.

3. Preheat the Air Fryer:
   - Preheat your air fryer to 375°F (190°C) for about 3-5 minutes. Preheating ensures that the spring rolls start cooking immediately, achieving a crispy exterior.

4. Air Fry the Spring Rolls:
- Place the prepared spring rolls in the air fryer basket, ensuring they are not touching. Cook for 5-6 minutes, turn the rolls, and continue to cook for an additional 5-6 minutes or until they are golden brown and crispy.

5. Check for Doneness:
- The spring rolls should be golden and crispy. If needed, cook for an additional 1-2 minutes for extra crispiness.

Serving:

- Serve these Crispy and Healthy Vegetarian Spring Rolls hot, accompanied by your favorite dipping sauce—soy sauce, sweet chili sauce, or a peanut dipping sauce. These spring rolls are perfect as appetizers, snacks, or as a light and flavorful addition to your meal.

CHAPTER 6
SAVORY GARLIC PARMESAN BRUSSELS SPROUTS

Get ready to transform humble Brussels sprouts into a culinary masterpiece with our Savory Garlic Parmesan Brussels Sprouts. In this chapter, we'll explore the art and science of air frying to elevate these green gems to a whole new level, creating a savory and crispy delight that will make Brussels sprouts the star of your table.

Ingredients:

- 1 pound Brussels sprouts, trimmed and halved
- 2 tablespoons olive oil
- 3 cloves garlic, minced
- 1/2 cup grated Parmesan cheese
- 1 teaspoon dried thyme
- Salt and black pepper, to taste
- Lemon wedges, for serving

Air Fryer Machine Settings:

- Preheat your air fryer to 375°F (190°C). Preheating ensures that the Brussels sprouts begin cooking immediately, resulting in a perfect combination of crispy exteriors and tender interiors.

Time:

- Cook the Brussels sprouts for 12-15 minutes, shaking or stirring halfway through. This method ensures even cooking and the development of a golden, cheesy crust.

Method:

1. Prepare the Brussels Sprouts:
- Trim the ends of the Brussels sprouts and cut them in half. Remove any loose or discolored outer leaves.

2. Season and Toss:
   - In a large bowl, toss the Brussels sprouts with olive oil, minced garlic, grated Parmesan cheese, dried thyme, salt, and black pepper. Ensure that the Brussels sprouts are evenly coated with the flavorful mixture.

3. Preheat the Air Fryer:
   - Preheat your air fryer to 375°F (190°C) for about 3-5 minutes. Preheating sets the stage for achieving the desired crispiness while allowing the garlic and Parmesan to adhere to the sprouts.

4. Air Fry the Brussels Sprouts:
   - Place the seasoned Brussels sprouts in the air fryer basket, spreading them out for even cooking. Cook for 6-8 minutes, shake or stir the sprouts, and continue to cook for an additional 6-8 minutes or until they are golden brown and crispy.

5. Check for Doneness:
   - The Brussels sprouts should be golden and crispy on the outside while remaining tender on the inside. Adjust the cooking time if needed for your desired level of crispiness.

Serving:

- Serve these Savory Garlic Parmesan Brussels Sprouts hot, with a squeeze of fresh lemon juice for brightness. Whether as a delightful side dish or a flavorful snack, these sprouts are bound to become a favorite at your table.

Congratulations on exploring the world of Brussels sprouts with your air fryer. Get ready to savor more culinary wonders in the upcoming chapters of "Air Fryer Recipe Instructor." Happy air frying!

CHAPTER 7:
HOMEMADE CRISPY ONION RINGS

In this chapter, we embark on a journey to unveil the secrets behind crafting the perfect Homemade Crispy Onion Rings using the magic of your air fryer. Get ready to experience the satisfaction of biting into a golden, crunchy exterior that encases the sweetness of perfectly cooked onions. Let's dive into the art and science of creating this classic, crowd-pleasing snack.

Ingredients:

- 2 large yellow onions, sliced into rings
- 1 cup all-purpose flour
- 1 teaspoon garlic powder
- 1 teaspoon paprika
- 1/2 teaspoon baking powder
- 1 cup buttermilk
- 1 cup breadcrumbs (preferably panko)
- Salt and black pepper, to taste

- Cooking spray or olive oil spray

Air Fryer Machine Settings:

- Preheat your air fryer to 375°F (190°C). Preheating ensures a quick and even cooking process, resulting in the perfect crispy exterior.

Time:

- Cook the onion rings for 8-10 minutes, flipping halfway through. This method ensures that each ring achieves that coveted golden brown and crunchy texture.

Method:

1. Prepare the Onions:
- Slice the onions into rings and separate them. For uniform cooking, choose onions of similar size.

2. Create the Dredging Station:
   - Set up a dredging station with three bowls. In the first bowl, place flour, garlic powder, paprika, baking powder, salt, and black pepper. In the second bowl, pour the buttermilk. In the third bowl, place breadcrumbs.

3. Dredge the Onion Rings:
   - Dredge each onion ring in the flour mixture, dip it into the buttermilk, and coat it with breadcrumbs. Ensure an even coating for a uniform and crispy result.

4. Preheat the Air Fryer:
   - Preheat your air fryer to 375°F (190°C) for about 3-5 minutes. Preheating ensures that the onion rings start cooking immediately, achieving that perfect crunch.

5. Air Fry the Onion Rings:

- Place the prepared onion rings in the air fryer basket, making sure they are not crowded. Cook for 4-5 minutes, flip the rings, and continue to cook for an additional 4-5 minutes or until they are golden brown and crispy.

6. Check for Doneness:
- The onion rings should be golden and crispy on the outside, with the onion inside cooked to a tender perfection. Adjust the cooking time if needed.

Serving:

- Serve these Homemade Crispy Onion Rings hot, perhaps with a side of your favorite dipping sauce—ranch, ketchup, or a spicy aioli. Whether as an appetizer, snack, or a crunchy addition to your burger, these onion rings are a testament to the joy of air frying.

CHAPTER 8
SPICY SWEET POTATO FRIES

In this chapter, we explore the delightful combination of sweet and spicy flavors as we learn to craft the perfect Spicy Sweet Potato Fries using the air fryer. Get ready to indulge in a delicious and nutritious snack that balances the natural sweetness of sweet potatoes with a hint of spice, all while achieving that coveted crispiness.

Ingredients:

- 2 large sweet potatoes, peeled and cut into matchsticks
- 2 tablespoons olive oil
- 1 teaspoon smoked paprika
- 1/2 teaspoon cayenne pepper (adjust to taste)
- 1 teaspoon garlic powder
- 1 teaspoon onion powder
- Salt and black pepper, to taste

- Fresh cilantro, chopped, for garnish

Air Fryer Machine Settings:

- Preheat your air fryer to 400°F (200°C). Preheating ensures a quick and even cooking process, resulting in perfectly crispy sweet potato fries.

Time:

- Cook the sweet potato fries for 15-18 minutes, shaking or stirring halfway through. This method ensures that each fry is evenly coated with the spicy seasoning and achieves the desired crispiness.

Method:

1. Prepare the Sweet Potatoes:
- Peel and cut the sweet potatoes into matchsticks, ensuring they are of similar size for uniform cooking.

2. Season the Fries:
   - In a large bowl, toss the sweet potato matchsticks with olive oil, smoked paprika, cayenne pepper, garlic powder, onion powder, salt, and black pepper. Ensure that each fry is evenly coated with the flavorful mixture.

3. Preheat the Air Fryer:
   - Preheat your air fryer to 400°F (200°C) for about 3-5 minutes. Preheating allows the sweet potato fries to start cooking immediately, contributing to that perfect balance of sweetness and spice.

4. Air Fry the Sweet Potato Fries:
   - Place the seasoned sweet potato fries in the air fryer basket, ensuring they are in a single layer for even cooking. Cook for 8-9 minutes, shake or stir the fries, and continue to cook for an additional 7-9 minutes or until they are golden brown and crispy.

5. Check for Doneness:
- The sweet potato fries should be golden and crispy on the outside while remaining tender on the inside. Adjust the cooking time if needed for your desired level of crispiness.

Serving:

- Serve these Spicy Sweet Potato Fries hot, garnished with fresh cilantro for a burst of freshness. Whether as a snack, a side dish, or a unique appetizer, these fries are sure to tantalize your taste buds with the perfect blend of sweet and spicy.

Congratulations on mastering the art and science of balancing flavors in your air-fried Spicy Sweet Potato Fries. Get ready to explore more culinary wonders in the upcoming chapters of "Air Fryer Recipe Instructor." Happy air frying!

CHAPTER 9
AIR-FRIED BBQ CHICKEN DRUMSTICKS

In this chapter, we'll delve into the mastery of infusing smoky barbecue flavor into succulent chicken drumsticks using the convenience of your air fryer. Get ready to elevate your barbecue game and enjoy the richness of perfectly cooked drumsticks with a deliciously crisp exterior.

Ingredients:

- 8 chicken drumsticks
- 1 cup barbecue sauce (your favorite brand or homemade)
- 2 tablespoons olive oil
- 1 teaspoon smoked paprika
- 1 teaspoon garlic powder
- 1 teaspoon onion powder
- Salt and black pepper, to taste
- Fresh parsley, chopped, for garnish

Air Fryer Machine Settings:

- Preheat your air fryer to 400°F (200°C). Preheating ensures a quick and even cooking process, allowing the drumsticks to develop a crispy exterior while absorbing the barbecue flavors.

Time:

- Cook the chicken drumsticks for 25-30 minutes, turning halfway through. This method ensures the drumsticks are cooked evenly and acquire that smoky barbecue essence.

Method:

1. Prepare the Chicken Drumsticks:
- Pat the drumsticks dry with paper towels. This step is crucial for achieving crispy skin on the air-fried drumsticks.

2. Season the Drumsticks:
   - In a bowl, mix together olive oil, smoked paprika, garlic powder, onion powder, salt, and black pepper. Brush this mixture over each drumstick, ensuring they are evenly coated.

3. Preheat the Air Fryer:
   - Preheat your air fryer to 400°F (200°C) for about 3-5 minutes. Preheating is essential for starting the cooking process immediately and creating that desirable crispy texture.

4. Air Fry the BBQ Chicken Drumsticks:
   - Place the seasoned drumsticks in the air fryer basket, ensuring they are not crowded. Cook for 12-15 minutes, turn the drumsticks, and continue to cook for an additional 12-15 minutes or until they reach an internal temperature of 165°F (74°C).

5. Brush with Barbecue Sauce:

- About halfway through the cooking time, brush each drumstick generously with barbecue sauce. This step allows the sauce to caramelize, enhancing the smoky flavor.

6. Check for Doneness:
- Ensure the drumsticks are cooked through, and the skin is crispy. The barbecue sauce should be sticky and well-glazed.

Serving:

- Serve these Air-Fried BBQ Chicken Drumsticks hot, garnished with chopped fresh parsley. Pair them with your favorite side dishes—coleslaw, baked beans, or corn on the cob. Whether for a family meal or a barbecue gathering, these drumsticks are a testament to the delicious possibilities that your air fryer offers.

CHAPTER 10
CRISPY COCONUT SHRIMP

Transport your taste buds to the tropics with the delightful combination of crispy coconut and succulent shrimp, all crafted effortlessly in your air fryer. In this chapter, we'll explore the art and science of creating Crispy Coconut Shrimp—a tropical delight that captures the essence of sunshine and sandy beaches.

Ingredients:

For the Coconut Shrimp:

- 1 pound large shrimp, peeled and deveined
- 1 cup shredded coconut (unsweetened)
- 1 cup panko breadcrumbs
- 2 eggs, beaten
- 1/2 cup all-purpose flour
- 1 teaspoon garlic powder
- 1 teaspoon onion powder
- Salt and black pepper, to taste

For the Dipping Sauce:

- 1/2 cup apricot preserves
- 2 tablespoons Dijon mustard
- 1 tablespoon soy sauce
- 1 teaspoon rice vinegar
- 1 teaspoon grated ginger

Air Fryer Machine Settings:

- Preheat your air fryer to 375°F (190°C). Preheating ensures a quick and even cooking process, allowing the coconut shrimp to achieve a perfect golden crisp.

Time:

- Cook the coconut shrimp for 8-10 minutes, turning halfway through. This method ensures each shrimp is evenly coated and achieves the desired level of crispiness.

Method:

1. Prepare the Coconut Shrimp:
- In a shallow bowl, mix together shredded coconut, panko breadcrumbs, garlic powder, onion powder, salt, and black pepper.

2. Dredge the Shrimp:
- Coat each shrimp in flour, dip into beaten eggs, and then coat with the coconut mixture. Ensure each shrimp is well-covered with the coconut and breadcrumb mixture.

3. Preheat the Air Fryer:
- Preheat your air fryer to 375°F (190°C) for about 3-5 minutes. Preheating sets the stage for achieving that perfect balance of a crispy exterior and juicy interior.

4. Air Fry the Coconut Shrimp:
- Place the coated shrimp in the air fryer basket, ensuring they are not overcrowded. Cook for 4-

5 minutes, turn the shrimp, and continue to cook for an additional 4-5 minutes or until they are golden brown and crispy.

5. Prepare the Dipping Sauce:
- While the shrimp are cooking, mix together apricot preserves, Dijon mustard, soy sauce, rice vinegar, and grated ginger in a small bowl. This dipping sauce complements the coconut shrimp with a perfect balance of sweet and tangy flavors.

6. Check for Doneness:
- The coconut shrimp should be golden brown and crispy on the outside, with the shrimp cooked through and tender on the inside.

Serving:

- Serve these Crispy Coconut Shrimp hot, accompanied by the tantalizing apricot dipping sauce. Whether as an appetizer, part of a tropical-themed meal, or a delightful snack, these coconut shrimp bring a taste of paradise to your table.

CHAPTER 11

MOUTHWATERING TERIYAKI SALMON

Embark on a journey of flavor fusion as we explore the art of air-frying Teriyaki-Glazed Salmon, creating a mouthwatering dinner option that combines the richness of salmon with the savory-sweet notes of teriyaki. In this chapter, we'll delve into the nuances of achieving perfectly cooked and glazed salmon fillets in your air fryer.

Ingredients:

- 4 salmon fillets
- 1/2 cup soy sauce

- 1/4 cup mirin (Japanese sweet rice wine)
- 2 tablespoons sake (or white wine)
- 2 tablespoons brown sugar
- 1 tablespoon honey
- 1 tablespoon grated ginger
- 2 cloves garlic, minced
- 1 tablespoon sesame oil
- Green onions, sliced, for garnish
- Sesame seeds, for garnish

Air Fryer Machine Settings:

- Preheat your air fryer to 400°F (200°C). Preheating ensures a quick and even cooking process, allowing the teriyaki glaze to caramelize on the salmon.

Time:

- Cook the salmon for 10-12 minutes, basting with teriyaki sauce halfway through. This method ensures that the salmon is perfectly cooked and infused with the irresistible teriyaki flavors.

Method:

1. Prepare the Teriyaki Sauce:
- In a saucepan, combine soy sauce, mirin, sake, brown sugar, honey, grated ginger, minced garlic, and sesame oil. Simmer over medium heat, stirring occasionally, until the sauce thickens slightly. Set aside a portion for basting.

2. Marinate the Salmon:
- Place the salmon fillets in a shallow dish and brush them with a generous amount of teriyaki sauce, ensuring each fillet is well-coated. Allow the salmon to marinate for at least 15 minutes, allowing the flavors to permeate.

3. Preheat the Air Fryer:
- Preheat your air fryer to 400°F (200°C) for about 3-5 minutes. Preheating is essential for the

teriyaki glaze to quickly caramelize, creating a flavorful crust on the salmon.

4. Air Fry the Teriyaki Salmon:
- Place the marinated salmon fillets in the air fryer basket, ensuring they are not overcrowded. Cook for 5-6 minutes, baste the fillets with the reserved teriyaki sauce, and continue to cook for an additional 5-6 minutes or until the salmon is cooked to your liking.

5. Check for Doneness:
- The salmon should be opaque and flake easily with a fork. The teriyaki glaze should have caramelized, creating a beautiful sheen on the fillets.

Serving:

- Serve this Mouthwatering Teriyaki Salmon hot, garnished with sliced green onions and sesame seeds. Pair it with steamed rice, stir-fried vegetables, or a light salad for a complete and delectable dinner option.

CHAPTER 12
STUFFED PORTOBELLO MUSHROOMS

In this chapter, we'll delve into the world of Stuffed Portobello Mushrooms, a savory and satisfying dish that showcases the versatility of your air fryer. Get ready to explore the art and science of creating a flavorful stuffing nestled within the rich and earthy embrace of Portobello mushrooms.

Ingredients:

- 4 large Portobello mushrooms, stems removed
- 1 cup cooked quinoa or couscous
- 1 cup spinach, chopped
- 1/2 cup sun-dried tomatoes, chopped

- 1/2 cup feta cheese, crumbled
- 2 cloves garlic, minced
- 2 tablespoons olive oil
- 1 teaspoon dried oregano
- Salt and black pepper, to taste
- Fresh parsley, chopped, for garnish

Air Fryer Machine Settings:

- Preheat your air fryer to 375°F (190°C). Preheating ensures an even cooking process, allowing the stuffed mushrooms to cook to perfection.

Time:

- Cook the stuffed mushrooms for 12-15 minutes. This method ensures the mushrooms are tender, and the stuffing is heated through.

Method:

1. Prepare the Portobello Mushrooms:

- Remove the stems from the Portobello mushrooms, creating a cavity for the stuffing. Lightly brush the mushrooms with olive oil and sprinkle with salt and black pepper.

2. Prepare the Stuffing:
- In a bowl, combine cooked quinoa or couscous, chopped spinach, sun-dried tomatoes, feta cheese, minced garlic, olive oil, dried oregano, salt, and black pepper. Mix the ingredients thoroughly.

3. Stuff the Mushrooms:
- Fill each Portobello mushroom with the prepared stuffing, pressing it down gently to ensure a well-packed and flavorful bite.

4. Preheat the Air Fryer:
- Preheat your air fryer to 375°F (190°C) for about 3-5 minutes. Preheating sets the stage for even cooking and ensures the mushrooms cook

through while maintaining their structural integrity.

5. Air Fry the Stuffed Portobello Mushrooms:
- Place the stuffed mushrooms in the air fryer basket, ensuring they are not crowded. Cook for 12-15 minutes or until the mushrooms are tender, and the stuffing is heated through.

6. Check for Doneness:
- The mushrooms should be tender when pierced with a fork, and the stuffing should be hot and flavorful.

Serving:

- Serve these Stuffed Portobello Mushrooms hot, garnished with fresh chopped parsley. Whether as a delightful appetizer or a meatless main course, these stuffed mushrooms are sure to impress with their rich flavors and satisfying texture.

CHAPTER 13

AIR-FRIED FALAFEL WITH TAHINI SAUCE

Discover the crispy goodness of falafel without the need for deep frying, as we explore the art and science of creating Air-Fried Falafel paired with a creamy and tangy Tahini Sauce. In this chapter, we'll embark on a culinary adventure, bringing you the flavors of the Middle East through the convenience of your air fryer.

Ingredients:

For the Falafel:

- 2 cans (30 oz) chickpeas, drained and rinsed
- 1 small onion, roughly chopped
- 4 cloves garlic, minced

- 1 cup fresh parsley, chopped
- 1 teaspoon ground cumin
- 1 teaspoon ground coriander
- 1/2 teaspoon cayenne pepper
- 1 teaspoon baking powder
- Salt and black pepper, to taste
- 2 tablespoons all-purpose flour
- Olive oil (for brushing)

For the Tahini Sauce:

- 1/2 cup tahini
- 2 tablespoons lemon juice
- 2 tablespoons water
- 1 clove garlic, minced
- Salt, to taste

Air Fryer Machine Settings:

- Preheat your air fryer to 375°F (190°C). Preheating ensures an even cooking process, allowing the falafel to develop a crisp exterior.

Time:

- Cook the falafel for 12-15 minutes, turning halfway through. This method ensures that each falafel achieves a golden brown and crispy texture.

Method:

1. Prepare the Falafel Mixture:
- In a food processor, combine chickpeas, chopped onion, minced garlic, fresh parsley, ground cumin, ground coriander, cayenne pepper, baking powder, salt, and black pepper. Pulse until the mixture forms a coarse paste.

2. Form the Falafel Balls:
- Transfer the falafel mixture to a bowl and add all-purpose flour. Mix until well combined. Shape the mixture into golf ball-sized falafel, ensuring they are compact and evenly shaped.

3. Preheat the Air Fryer:
   - Preheat your air fryer to 375°F (190°C) for about 3-5 minutes. Preheating ensures the falafel start cooking immediately, achieving that perfect crispy exterior.

4. Air Fry the Falafel:
   - Place the falafel in the air fryer basket, ensuring they are not overcrowded. Lightly brush each falafel with olive oil. Cook for 6-8 minutes, turn the falafel, and continue to cook for an additional 6-8 minutes or until they are golden brown and crispy.

5. Prepare the Tahini Sauce:
   - While the falafel are cooking, mix together tahini, lemon juice, water, minced garlic, and salt in a bowl. Adjust the consistency with water as needed.

6. Check for Doneness:
- The falafel should be golden brown on the outside and cooked through on the inside.

Serving:

- Serve these Air-Fried Falafel hot, accompanied by a generous drizzle of Tahini Sauce. Enjoy them in pita bread, on a salad, or as part of a mezze platter. The creamy tahini sauce complements the crispy falafel, creating a perfect harmony of flavors.

CHAPTER 14

CAJUN SPICED SWEET POTATO CHIPS

Elevate your snack game with a burst of flavor and a hint of spice as we explore the creation of Cajun Spiced Sweet Potato Chips in your air fryer. In this chapter, we'll delve into the art and science of transforming sweet potatoes into crispy, Cajun-spiced delights for a flavorful and healthy treat.

Ingredients:

- 2 large sweet potatoes, thinly sliced
- 2 tablespoons olive oil
- 1 teaspoon smoked paprika
- 1 teaspoon onion powder
- 1 teaspoon garlic powder
- 1/2 teaspoon cayenne pepper (adjust to taste)
- 1 teaspoon dried thyme
- Salt and black pepper, to taste
- Fresh parsley, chopped, for garnish

Air Fryer Machine Settings:

- Preheat your air fryer to 375°F (190°C). Preheating ensures an even cooking process, allowing the sweet potato chips to achieve the perfect balance of crispiness and tenderness.

Time:

- Cook the sweet potato chips for 12-15 minutes, shaking or stirring halfway through. This method ensures each chip is evenly coated with the Cajun spice mixture and reaches the desired level of crispiness.

Method:

1. Prepare the Sweet Potato Chips:
- Wash and peel the sweet potatoes. Using a mandoline or a sharp knife, thinly slice the sweet potatoes into uniform rounds.

2. Season the Chips:
   - In a large bowl, toss the sweet potato slices with olive oil, smoked paprika, onion powder, garlic powder, cayenne pepper, dried thyme, salt, and black pepper. Ensure each slice is evenly coated with the Cajun spice mixture.

3. Preheat the Air Fryer:
   - Preheat your air fryer to 375°F (190°C) for about 3-5 minutes. Preheating is crucial for the sweet potato chips to start cooking immediately, resulting in a perfect blend of crispy exteriors and tender interiors.

4. Air Fry the Sweet Potato Chips:
   - Place the seasoned sweet potato chips in the air fryer basket, ensuring they are in a single layer for even cooking. Cook for 6-8 minutes, shake or stir the chips, and continue to cook for an additional 6-8 minutes or until they are golden brown and crispy.

5. Check for Doneness:
- The sweet potato chips should be golden and crispy, with a slight curl at the edges. Adjust the cooking time if needed for your desired level of crispiness.

Serving:

- Serve these Cajun Spiced Sweet Potato Chips hot, garnished with chopped fresh parsley. Whether as a standalone snack or a side dish for your favorite meal, these chips are a flavorful and healthy alternative to traditional potato chips.

Congratulations on spicing up your snack game with Cajun Spiced Sweet Potato Chips. Get ready to savor more culinary wonders in the upcoming chapters of "Air Fryer Recipe Instructor." Happy air frying!

CHAPTER 15
LEMON GARLIC PARMESAN ASPARAGUS

In this chapter, we'll showcase the versatility of your air fryer by preparing a delightful side dish of Lemon Garlic Parmesan Asparagus. Get ready to experience the perfect balance of tenderness and crispiness in each vibrant asparagus spear, elevated with the zesty flavors of lemon, savory garlic, and Parmesan cheese.

Ingredients:

- 1 bunch asparagus, tough ends trimmed
- 2 tablespoons olive oil
- Zest of 1 lemon
- 2 cloves garlic, minced
- 1/4 cup grated Parmesan cheese
- Salt and black pepper, to taste
- Fresh parsley, chopped, for garnish
- Lemon wedges, for serving

Air Fryer Machine Settings:

- Preheat your air fryer to 400°F (200°C). Preheating ensures a quick and even cooking process, allowing the asparagus to achieve a delightful crispness while retaining its tenderness.

Time:

- Cook the asparagus for 8-10 minutes, shaking or stirring halfway through. This method ensures that each asparagus spear is evenly coated with the lemon garlic Parmesan mixture and reaches the perfect level of crispiness.

Method:

1. Prepare the Asparagus:
- Trim the tough ends of the asparagus spears, leaving the tender tips intact. If needed, peel

the lower part of the asparagus for a more even texture.

2. Create the Lemon Garlic Parmesan Mixture:
- In a bowl, combine olive oil, lemon zest, minced garlic, grated Parmesan cheese, salt, and black pepper. Mix the ingredients until well combined.

3. Coat the Asparagus:
- Toss the trimmed asparagus spears in the lemon garlic Parmesan mixture, ensuring each spear is evenly coated.

4. Preheat the Air Fryer:
- Preheat your air fryer to 400°F (200°C) for about 3-5 minutes. Preheating sets the stage for achieving the perfect balance of crispiness and tenderness in the asparagus.

5. Air Fry the Asparagus:
- Place the coated asparagus spears in the air fryer basket, ensuring they are not overcrowded. Cook for 4-5 minutes, shake or stir the asparagus, and continue to cook for an additional 4-5 minutes or until they are vibrant green and crispy.

6. Check for Doneness:
- The asparagus should be tender yet crisp, with the Parmesan cheese forming a golden crust.

Serving:

- Serve this Lemon Garlic Parmesan Asparagus hot, garnished with chopped fresh parsley and accompanied by lemon wedges. Whether as a vibrant side dish for a formal dinner or a quick weeknight meal, this flavorful asparagus will elevate any dining experience.

CHAPTER 16

CRISPY COCONUT CHICKEN TENDERS

Elevate the classic chicken tenders to new heights by infusing them with a delightful tropical twist. In this chapter, we'll explore the art and science of creating Crispy Coconut Chicken Tenders in your air fryer, bringing together the succulence of tender chicken with the exotic crunch of coconut.

Ingredients:

- 1.5 pounds chicken tenders
- 1 cup shredded coconut (unsweetened)
- 1 cup panko breadcrumbs
- 2 eggs, beaten
- 1/2 cup all-purpose flour
- 1 teaspoon garlic powder
- 1 teaspoon onion powder
- 1/2 teaspoon smoked paprika
- Salt and black pepper, to taste

- Sweet chili sauce, for dipping

Air Fryer Machine Settings:

- Preheat your air fryer to 375°F (190°C). Preheating is essential for achieving an even and crispy coating on the chicken tenders.

Time:

- Cook the chicken tenders for 12-15 minutes, turning halfway through. This method ensures each tender is evenly coated with the coconut and achieves the desired level of crispiness.

Method:

1. Prepare the Chicken Tenders:
- Pat the chicken tenders dry with paper towels to ensure optimal coating. Season with salt, black pepper, garlic powder, and onion powder.

2. Set Up Breading Stations:
- In one bowl, place all-purpose flour. In another bowl, beat the eggs. In a third bowl, combine shredded coconut, panko breadcrumbs, smoked paprika, and additional salt to taste.

3. Coat the Chicken Tenders:
- Dredge each chicken tender in flour, ensuring an even coating. Dip in the beaten eggs, then coat generously with the coconut and breadcrumb mixture, pressing the coating onto the chicken to adhere.

4. Preheat the Air Fryer:
- Preheat your air fryer to 375°F (190°C) for about 3-5 minutes. Preheating is crucial for starting the cooking process immediately and achieving that perfect balance of a crispy exterior and juicy interior.

5. Air Fry the Coconut Chicken Tenders:

- Place the coated chicken tenders in the air fryer basket, ensuring they are not overcrowded. Cook for 6-8 minutes, turn the tenders, and continue to cook for an additional 6-8 minutes or until they are golden brown and crispy.

6. Check for Doneness:
- The chicken tenders should be golden brown with a crispy coconut coating and cooked through to perfection.

Serving:

- Serve these Crispy Coconut Chicken Tenders hot, accompanied by a side of sweet chili sauce for dipping. Whether as a delightful appetizer or the main course of a tropical-themed meal, these chicken tenders bring a taste of paradise to your table.

CHAPTER 17
MANGO SALSA STUFFED AVOCADO

In this chapter, we'll explore the refreshing combination of Mango Salsa Stuffed Avocado, showcasing the air fryer's ability to enhance flavors and textures. Immerse yourself in the fusion of creamy avocado and vibrant mango salsa, creating a dish that's not only visually appealing but also bursting with fresh and zesty flavors.

Ingredients:

- 2 ripe avocados, halved and pitted
- 1 cup diced mango
- 1/2 cup diced red onion
- 1/2 cup cherry tomatoes, diced
- 1/4 cup fresh cilantro, chopped
- Juice of 1 lime
- Salt and black pepper, to taste
- Optional: Jalapeño, diced (for a spicy kick)

Air Fryer Machine Settings:

- Preheat your air fryer to 375°F (190°C). Preheating ensures a quick and even warming of the avocados, allowing the mango salsa to complement their creamy texture.

Time:

- Warm the avocado halves for 2-3 minutes. This brief warming period enhances the overall dish by adding a touch of warmth to the avocados.

Method:

1. Prepare the Mango Salsa:
- In a bowl, combine diced mango, red onion, cherry tomatoes, fresh cilantro, lime juice, salt, black pepper, and optional diced jalapeño if you desire a spicy kick. Mix the ingredients until well combined.

2. Halve and Pit the Avocados:
   - Cut the avocados in half, remove the pits, and scoop out a small portion of the flesh to create a well for the salsa.

3. Fill the Avocado Halves:
   - Spoon the prepared mango salsa into the wells of the avocado halves, ensuring they are generously filled with the vibrant and flavorful mixture.

4. Preheat the Air Fryer:
   - Preheat your air fryer to 375°F (190°C) for about 3-5 minutes. Preheating ensures the avocados are warmed through without compromising their creamy texture.

5. Warm the Avocado Halves:
   - Place the stuffed avocado halves in the air fryer basket. Warm them for 2-3 minutes, allowing

the avocados to absorb a touch of warmth, enhancing the overall eating experience.

6. Check for Doneness:
- The avocados should be warmed through but still maintain their creamy texture. The mango salsa on top should remain fresh and vibrant.

Serving:

- Serve these Mango Salsa Stuffed Avocado halves immediately, garnished with additional cilantro if desired. Whether as a refreshing appetizer or a light meal, this dish is a testament to the air fryer's ability to elevate the simplest ingredients into a culinary masterpiece.

CHAPTER 18
GARLIC HERB ROASTED POTATOES

In this chapter, we'll delve into the art of achieving the perfect balance of crispy and tender with Garlic Herb Roasted Potatoes made in the air fryer. Discover how the air fryer transforms humble potatoes into golden, flavorful bites, showcasing the mastery of textures and flavors.

Ingredients:

- 2 pounds baby potatoes, halved or quartered
- 2 tablespoons olive oil
- 4 cloves garlic, minced
- 1 teaspoon dried thyme
- 1 teaspoon dried rosemary
- 1 teaspoon dried oregano
- Salt and black pepper, to taste
- Fresh parsley, chopped, for garnish

Air Fryer Machine Settings:

- Preheat your air fryer to 400°F (200°C). Preheating ensures a quick and even cooking process, allowing the potatoes to achieve the perfect balance of crispiness and tenderness.

Time:

- Cook the potatoes for 20-25 minutes, shaking or stirring halfway through. This method ensures each potato is evenly coated with the garlic herb mixture and reaches the desired level of crispiness.

Method:

1. Prepare the Potatoes:
- Wash and halve or quarter the baby potatoes, depending on their size. Pat them dry with a paper towel to remove excess moisture.

2. Create the Garlic Herb Mixture:

- In a bowl, combine olive oil, minced garlic, dried thyme, dried rosemary, dried oregano, salt, and black pepper. Mix the ingredients until they form a fragrant herb-infused oil.

3. Coat the Potatoes:
- Toss the potatoes in the garlic herb mixture, ensuring each piece is evenly coated. The oil and herbs will contribute to both the crispiness and flavor of the roasted potatoes.

4. Preheat the Air Fryer:
- Preheat your air fryer to 400°F (200°C) for about 3-5 minutes. Preheating is essential for starting the cooking process immediately, ensuring the potatoes achieve that perfect balance of crispiness and tenderness.

5. Air Fry the Potatoes:
- Place the coated potatoes in the air fryer basket, ensuring they are in a single layer for

even cooking. Cook for 10-12 minutes, shake or stir the potatoes, and continue to cook for an additional 10-12 minutes or until they are golden brown and crispy.

6. Check for Doneness:
- The potatoes should be golden brown with a crispy exterior and a tender interior.

Serving:

- Serve these Garlic Herb Roasted Potatoes hot, garnished with chopped fresh parsley. Whether as a side dish for a hearty meal or a standalone snack, these potatoes showcase the air fryer's ability to master the art of achieving the perfect balance of textures and flavors.

CHAPTER 19
BUFFALO CAULIFLOWER BITES

Experience the bold and tangy flavors of buffalo sauce with a healthier twist in this chapter, as we air-fry cauliflower bites to crispy perfection. Dive into the world of Buffalo Cauliflower Bites, where the art and science of air frying combine to create a mouthwatering and guilt-free snack.

Ingredients:

- 1 medium-sized cauliflower, cut into florets
- 1 cup all-purpose flour
- 1 cup milk (or plant-based alternative)
- 1 teaspoon garlic powder
- 1 teaspoon onion powder
- 1/2 teaspoon smoked paprika
- 1/2 teaspoon salt
- 1/4 teaspoon black pepper
- 1 cup buffalo sauce

- 2 tablespoons melted butter (optional, for added richness)
- Green onions, sliced, for garnish
- Ranch or blue cheese dressing, for dipping

Air Fryer Machine Settings:

- Preheat your air fryer to 375°F (190°C). Preheating ensures the cauliflower bites start cooking immediately, resulting in a perfect balance of crispiness and tenderness.

Time:

- Cook the cauliflower bites for 15-18 minutes, shaking or stirring halfway through. This method ensures each bite is evenly coated with the buffalo sauce and reaches the desired level of crispiness.

Method:

1. Prepare the Cauliflower Bites:

- Cut the cauliflower into florets, ensuring they are of similar size for even cooking. Set aside.

2. Create the Batter:
- In a bowl, whisk together all-purpose flour, milk, garlic powder, onion powder, smoked paprika, salt, and black pepper. The batter should be smooth and thick enough to coat the cauliflower.

3. Coat the Cauliflower:
- Dip each cauliflower floret into the batter, ensuring an even coating. Allow any excess batter to drip off.

4. Preheat the Air Fryer:
- Preheat your air fryer to 375°F (190°C) for about 3-5 minutes. Preheating is crucial for achieving the perfect balance of crispiness and tenderness in the cauliflower bites.

5. Air Fry the Cauliflower Bites:
- Place the coated cauliflower bites in the air fryer basket, ensuring they are not overcrowded. Cook for 7-9 minutes, shake or stir the bites, and continue to cook for an additional 7-9 minutes or until they are golden brown and crispy.

6. Prepare the Buffalo Sauce:
- While the cauliflower bites are air frying, mix buffalo sauce and melted butter in a bowl. Adjust the butter amount to your desired richness.

7. Coat the Cauliflower in Buffalo Sauce:
- Once the cauliflower bites are crispy, toss them in the prepared buffalo sauce mixture until evenly coated.

8. Check for Doneness:

- The cauliflower bites should be golden brown with a crispy exterior and a tender interior, coated in the flavorful buffalo sauce.

Serving:

- Serve these Buffalo Cauliflower Bites hot, garnished with sliced green onions, and accompanied by ranch or blue cheese dressing for dipping. Whether as a party snack or a game-day treat, these bites offer a healthier alternative to traditional buffalo wings without compromising on flavor.

Congratulations on experiencing the bold flavors of Buffalo Cauliflower Bites with your air fryer. Get ready to savor more culinary wonders in the upcoming chapters of "Air Fryer Recipe Instructor." Happy air frying!

CHAPTER 20
CHOCOLATE LAVA CAKE SURPRISE

Conclude your air frying journey on a sweet note with the mastery of creating a gooey and indulgent Chocolate Lava Cake. In this final chapter, we'll explore the art and science behind achieving the perfect molten center and rich chocolaty exterior, delivering a delightful surprise with every bite.

Ingredients:

- 1/2 cup unsalted butter
- 4 ounces high-quality dark chocolate, coarsely chopped
- 2 large eggs
- 2 large egg yolks
- 1/4 cup granulated sugar
- 1 teaspoon vanilla extract
- 1/4 cup all-purpose flour
- Pinch of salt

- Optional: Powdered sugar, berries, or vanilla ice cream for garnish

Air Fryer Machine Settings:

- Preheat your air fryer to 375°F (190°C). Preheating ensures the lava cakes start cooking immediately, resulting in a perfect balance of a molten center and a lightly crisped exterior.

Time:

- Cook the lava cakes for 8-10 minutes. This brief cooking time ensures the center remains gooey while the outer layer achieves a light, cake-like texture.

Method:

1. Prepare the Chocolate and Butter Mixture:
- In a heatproof bowl, melt the unsalted butter and coarsely chopped dark chocolate together. You can use a double boiler or melt in the

microwave in short intervals, stirring until smooth. Let it cool slightly.

2. Whisk the Eggs and Sugar:
- In a separate bowl, whisk together the eggs, egg yolks, granulated sugar, and vanilla extract until well combined and slightly frothy.

3. Combine the Chocolate Mixtures:
- Slowly pour the melted chocolate mixture into the egg mixture, stirring continuously to avoid scrambling the eggs. Ensure a smooth and homogeneous batter.

4. Add Flour and Salt:
- Gently fold in the all-purpose flour and a pinch of salt until just combined. Be careful not to over mix; the batter should be smooth.

5. Preheat the Air Fryer:

- Preheat your air fryer to 375°F (190°C) for about 3-5 minutes. Preheating is essential for achieving the perfect balance of a molten center and a lightly crisped exterior.

6. Fill the Ramekins:
- Grease individual ramekins and fill each with the chocolate batter. Leave some space at the top to allow for rising during cooking.

7. Air Fry the Lava Cakes:
- Place the filled ramekins in the air fryer basket, ensuring they are not overcrowded. Cook for 8-10 minutes, allowing the edges to set while keeping the center gooey.

8. Check for Doneness:
- The lava cakes should have a firm exterior while remaining molten in the center. Insert a toothpick, and it should come out with moist crumbs but not wet batter.

Serving:

- Serve these Chocolate Lava Cakes hot, either directly in the ramekins or inverted onto serving plates for a dramatic reveal. Dust with powdered sugar, garnish with berries, or serve with a scoop of vanilla ice cream for an extra indulgent treat.

CHAPTER 21
CAPRESE STUFFED PORTOBELLO MUSHROOMS

Explore the world of savory elegance with Caprese Stuffed Portobello Mushrooms. Learn how to create a flavorful dish by combining juicy tomatoes, fresh mozzarella, and basil inside hearty Portobello mushroom caps. The air fryer transforms this classic Italian combination into a warm and gooey delight.

Ingredients:

- 4 large Portobello mushrooms
- 1 cup cherry tomatoes, halved
- 1 cup fresh mozzarella, diced
- Fresh basil leaves, chopped
- Balsamic glaze, for drizzling
- Olive oil, for brushing
- Salt and black pepper, to taste

Air Fryer Machine Settings:

- Preheat your air fryer to 375°F (190°C).

Time:

- Cook for 10-12 minutes, until the mushrooms are tender and the cheese is melted.

CHAPTER 22

CINNAMON SUGAR APPLE CHIPS

Indulge your sweet tooth with a healthier twist.

Cinnamon Sugar Apple Chips combine the natural sweetness of apples with the warm flavors of cinnamon. Discover the perfect balance of crispy and sweet as you air fry these apple slices into a delightful snack.

Ingredients:

- 4 large apples, cored and thinly sliced
- 2 tablespoons cinnamon
- 2 tablespoons sugar

Air Fryer Machine Settings:

- Preheat your air fryer to 375°F (190°C).

Time:

- Cook for 8-10 minutes, flipping the slices halfway through, until they are golden brown.

CHAPTER 23
PESTO SHRIMP SKEWERS

Delight your taste buds with Pesto Shrimp Skewers that capture the essence of Mediterranean flavors. Learn the art of marinating shrimp in a vibrant pesto sauce and air frying them to perfection. These skewers make for a quick and flavorful seafood dish.

Ingredients:

- 1 pound large shrimp, peeled and deveined
- 1/2 cup basil pesto
- 1 lemon, juiced
- Salt and black pepper, to taste
- Wooden skewers, soaked in water

Air Fryer Machine Settings:

- Preheat your air fryer to 400°F (200°C).

Time:

- Cook for 6-8 minutes, turning the skewers halfway through, until the shrimp are opaque and lightly browned.

CHAPTER 24

MEDITERRANEAN STUFFED BELL PEPPERS

Embark on a journey to the Mediterranean with these flavorful Stuffed Bell Peppers. Discover the art of combining ground turkey, couscous, and a medley of vegetables, then air fry to perfection. These stuffed peppers are a wholesome and satisfying meal.

Ingredients:

- 4 large bell peppers, halved and seeds removed
- 1 pound ground turkey
- 1 cup cooked couscous
- 1 cup cherry tomatoes, diced
- 1/2 cup feta cheese, crumbled
- 1/4 cup kalamata olives, chopped
- 1 teaspoon dried oregano
- Salt and black pepper, to taste
- Olive oil, for drizzling

Air Fryer Machine Settings:

- Preheat your air fryer to 375°F (190°C).

Time:

- Cook for 15-18 minutes, until the peppers are tender and the filling is cooked through.

CHAPTER 25
TERIYAKI PINEAPPLE CHICKEN SKEWERS

Experience the perfect blend of sweet and savory with Teriyaki Pineapple Chicken Skewers. Master the art of marinating chicken and pineapple in a flavorful teriyaki sauce, then air fry for a mouthwatering dish that's both tender and delicious.

Ingredients:

- 1.5 pounds chicken breast, cut into cubes
- 1 cup pineapple chunks
- 1/2 cup teriyaki sauce
- 2 tablespoons soy sauce
- 1 tablespoon honey
- 1 teaspoon sesame oil

- Wooden skewers, soaked in water

Air Fryer Machine Settings:

- Preheat your air fryer to 375°F (190°C).

Time:

- Cook for 12-15 minutes, turning the skewers halfway through, until the chicken is cooked through and caramelized.

CHAPTER 26

SOUTHWEST STUFFED SWEET POTATOES

Discover the fusion of flavors with Southwest Stuffed Sweet Potatoes. Learn how to create a hearty and nutritious dish by air-frying sweet potatoes and filling them with a flavorful mixture of black beans, corn, avocado, and spices.

Ingredients:

- 4 medium-sized sweet potatoes
- 1 can (15 oz) black beans, drained and rinsed
- 1 cup corn kernels (fresh or frozen)
- 1 avocado, diced
- 1 cup cherry tomatoes, diced
- 1/4 cup red onion, finely chopped
- 1 teaspoon cumin
- 1 teaspoon chili powder
- Salt and black pepper, to taste

- Fresh cilantro, chopped, for garnish

Air Fryer Machine Settings:

- Preheat your air fryer to 400°F (200°C).

Time:

- Cook sweet potatoes for 30-35 minutes, until they are tender.

CHAPTER 27
LEMON HERB QUINOA CAKES

Elevate your plant-based cooking skills with Lemon Herb Quinoa Cakes. Learn how to blend quinoa with herbs and spices, then air fry to achieve a crispy exterior and a fluffy interior. These quinoa cakes make a delightful and protein-packed dish.

Ingredients:

- 2 cups cooked quinoa
- 1/2 cup breadcrumbs
- 1/4 cup nutritional yeast
- 2 tablespoons fresh lemon juice
- 1 tablespoon fresh parsley, chopped
- 1 teaspoon dried oregano
- 1 teaspoon garlic powder
- Salt and black pepper, to taste
- Olive oil, for brushing

Air Fryer Machine Settings:

- Preheat your air fryer to 375°F (190°C).

Time:

- Cook for 10-12 minutes, flipping the quinoa cakes halfway through, until they are golden brown.

CHAPTER 28
BALSAMIC GLAZED BRUSSELS SPROUTS

Transform Brussels sprouts into a savory and tangy delight with Balsamic Glazed Brussels Sprouts. Learn the art of caramelizing these cruciferous gems in the air fryer and drizzling them with a balsamic glaze for a flavorful side dish.

Ingredients:

- 1 pound Brussels sprouts, halved
- 2 tablespoons olive oil
- 2 tablespoons balsamic vinegar
- 1 tablespoon honey
- Salt and black pepper, to taste
- Crushed red pepper flakes, for a hint of spice

Air Fryer Machine Settings:

- Preheat your air fryer to 375°F (190°C).

Time:

- Cook for 15-18 minutes, shaking the basket halfway through, until the Brussels sprouts are caramelized and tender.

CHAPTER 29
PANKO-CRUSTED ZUCCHINI FRIES

Savor the crispiness of Panko-Crusted Zucchini Fries, a healthier alternative to traditional fries. Learn how to coat zucchini sticks in a seasoned Panko breadcrumb mixture and air fry them to perfection for a delicious snack or side dish.

Ingredients:

- 2 medium-sized zucchinis, cut into fries
- 1 cup Panko breadcrumbs
- 1/2 cup grated Parmesan cheese
- 1 teaspoon garlic powder
- 1 teaspoon dried Italian herbs
- Salt and black pepper, to taste
- Marinara sauce, for dipping

Air Fryer Machine Settings:

- Preheat your air fryer to 400°F (200°C).

Time:

- Cook for 10-12 minutes, shaking the basket halfway through, until the zucchini fries are golden and crispy.

CHAPTER 30
MAPLE GLAZED SALMON WITH ROASTED VEGETABLES

Master the art of preparing a complete meal in the air fryer with Maple Glazed Salmon and Roasted Vegetables. Learn how to coat salmon fillets with a sweet maple glaze and roast a medley of colorful vegetables for a wholesome and flavorful dinner.

Ingredients:

- 4 salmon fillets
- 1/4 cup maple syrup
- 2 tablespoons soy sauce
- 1 tablespoon Dijon mustard
- 1 teaspoon garlic powder
- 1 teaspoon dried thyme
- 1 pound mixed vegetables (such as bell peppers, carrots, and broccoli), chopped
- Olive oil, for drizzling
- Salt and black pepper, to taste

Air Fryer Machine Settings:

- Preheat your air fryer to 375°F (190°C).

Time:

- Cook for 12-15 minutes, flipping the salmon fillets and stirring the vegetables halfway through, until the salmon is cooked and the vegetables are tender.

CHAPTER 31
AVOCADO EGG ROLLS WITH SRIRACHA DIPPING SAUCE

Indulge in the crispy goodness of Avocado Egg Rolls, featuring a creamy avocado filling with a hint of spice. Learn how to roll and air fry these appetizers to perfection, and serve them with a zesty Sriracha dipping sauce.

Ingredients:

- 2 ripe avocados, mashed
- 1 cup red cabbage, thinly sliced
- 1 carrot, julienned
- 1/4 cup red onion, finely chopped
- 1 teaspoon lime juice
- 1 teaspoon soy sauce
- Egg roll wrappers
- Olive oil, for brushing

- Sriracha dipping sauce (mix Sriracha with mayo for desired spice level)

Air Fryer Machine Settings:

- Preheat your air fryer to 375°F (190°C).

Time:

- Cook for 8-10 minutes, until the egg rolls are golden brown and crispy.

CHAPTER 32
GREEK-STYLE STUFFED PEPPERS

Transport your taste buds to the Mediterranean with Greek-Style Stuffed Peppers. Discover how to fill bell peppers with a mixture of ground lamb, rice, and flavorful herbs, then air fry them for a satisfying and aromatic dish.

Ingredients:

- 4 large bell peppers, halved and seeds removed
- 1 pound ground lamb
- 1 cup cooked rice
- 1/2 cup feta cheese, crumbled
- 1/4 cup Kalamata olives, chopped
- 1 teaspoon dried oregano
- 1 teaspoon dried mint
- Salt and black pepper, to taste
- Olive oil, for drizzling

Air Fryer Machine Settings:

- Preheat your air fryer to 375°F (190°C).

Time:

- Cook for 15-18 minutes, until the peppers are tender and the filling is cooked through.

CHAPTER 33
ORANGE GLAZED CHICKEN DRUMSTICKS

Master the art of creating sticky and flavorful Orange Glazed Chicken Drumsticks. Learn how to marinate chicken drumsticks in a citrusy glaze and air fry them for a succulent and delicious result.

Ingredients:

- 2 pounds chicken drumsticks
- 1/2 cup orange marmalade
- 2 tablespoons soy sauce
- 1 tablespoon rice vinegar
- 1 teaspoon ginger, grated
- 1 teaspoon garlic, minced
- Sesame seeds and chopped green onions, for garnish

Air Fryer Machine Settings:

- Preheat your air fryer to 400°F (200°C).

Time:

- Cook for 20-25 minutes, turning the drumsticks halfway through, until they are golden and cooked through.

CHAPTER 34

SPINACH AND FETA STUFFED CHICKEN BREAST

Impress your guests with Spinach and Feta Stuffed Chicken Breast. Learn the technique of butterfly-cutting chicken breasts, stuffing them with a delicious spinach and feta mixture, and air frying to perfection.

Ingredients:

- 4 boneless, skinless chicken breasts
- 2 cups fresh spinach, chopped
- 1/2 cup feta cheese, crumbled
- 1/4 cup sun-dried tomatoes, chopped
- 1 teaspoon garlic powder
- 1 teaspoon dried oregano
- Salt and black pepper, to taste
- Olive oil, for brushing

Air Fryer Machine Settings:

- Preheat your air fryer to 375°F (190°C).

Time:

- Cook for 18-20 minutes, until the chicken is cooked through and the filling is hot.

CHAPTER 35

MAPLE BACON WRAPPED SHRIMP

Experience the perfect blend of sweet and savory with Maple Bacon Wrapped Shrimp. Learn how to wrap shrimp in bacon, brush them with a maple glaze, and air fry for a mouthwatering appetizer or snack.

Ingredients:

- 1 pound large shrimp, peeled and deveined
- 10-12 slices of bacon, cut in half
- 1/4 cup maple syrup
- 1 tablespoon Dijon mustard
- 1 teaspoon smoked paprika
- Toothpicks, for securing

Air Fryer Machine Settings:

- Preheat your air fryer to 375°F (190°C).

Time:

- Cook for 10-12 minutes, until the bacon is crispy and the shrimp are cooked through.

CHAPTER 36
TERIYAKI TOFU STIR-FRY

Explore the world of plant-based delights with Teriyaki Tofu Stir-Fry. Master the art of air-frying tofu to perfection and toss it in a flavorful teriyaki sauce with vibrant stir-fried vegetables. This dish is a balance of textures and tastes that will satisfy both vegetarians and meat lovers alike.

Ingredients:

- 1 block extra-firm tofu, pressed and cubed
- 2 cups broccoli florets
- 1 bell pepper, thinly sliced

- 1 carrot, julienned
- 1/2 cup snap peas
- 1/4 cup soy sauce
- 2 tablespoons teriyaki sauce
- 1 tablespoon sesame oil
- 1 tablespoon rice vinegar
- 1 tablespoon maple syrup
- Sesame seeds, for garnish
- Green onions, sliced, for garnish

Air Fryer Machine Settings:

- Preheat your air fryer to 375°F (190°C).

Time:

- Air-fry tofu for 15-18 minutes, shaking the basket halfway through.
- Stir-fry vegetables in a pan on the stovetop until tender-crisp.
- Toss tofu and vegetables in the teriyaki sauce mixture.

CHAPTER 37

TEX-MEX LOADED SWEET POTATO SKINS

Indulge in a fusion of flavors with Tex-Mex Loaded Sweet Potato Skins. Learn to air-fry sweet potato skins until crispy and then stuff them with a savory mixture of black beans, corn, and cheese for a delightful appetizer or side dish.

Ingredients:

- 4 medium-sized sweet potatoes, halved
- 1 can (15 oz) black beans, drained and rinsed
- 1 cup corn kernels (fresh or frozen)
- 1 cup shredded cheddar cheese
- 1 teaspoon chili powder
- 1 teaspoon cumin
- 1/2 teaspoon garlic powder
- 1/4 cup fresh cilantro, chopped

- Sour cream and sliced jalapeños, for garnish

Air Fryer Machine Settings:

- Preheat your air fryer to 400°F (200°C).

Time:

- Air-fry sweet potato skins for 18-20 minutes, until crispy.
- Fill with black bean and corn mixture, sprinkle with cheese, and air-fry for an additional 5 minutes.

CHAPTER 38
HAWAIIAN CHICKEN KABOBS

Embark on a tropical culinary journey with Hawaiian Chicken Kabobs. Learn how to marinate chicken in a pineapple-infused sauce, skewer them with colorful bell peppers and onions, and air-fry for a delicious and visually appealing dish.

Ingredients:

- 1.5 pounds chicken breast, cut into cubes
- 1 cup pineapple chunks
- 1 bell pepper, cut into chunks
- 1 red onion, cut into chunks
- 1/2 cup soy sauce
- 1/4 cup pineapple juice
- 2 tablespoons brown sugar
- 1 tablespoon sesame oil
- 1 teaspoon garlic powder
- Wooden skewers, soaked in water

Air Fryer Machine Settings:

- Preheat your air fryer to 375°F (190°C).

Time:

- Air-fry kabobs for 15-18 minutes, turning them halfway through, until the chicken is cooked through.

CHAPTER 39
LEMON BLUEBERRY MUFFINS

Indulge in a delightful dessert with Lemon Blueberry

Muffins. Learn how to create a light and fluffy muffin batter, infused with lemon zest and bursting with juicy blueberries, then air-fry for a quick and delectable treat.

Ingredients:

- 2 cups all-purpose flour
- 1/2 cup sugar
- 1 tablespoon baking powder
- 1/2 teaspoon salt
- 1 cup milk
- 1/4 cup vegetable oil
- 1 egg
- 1 teaspoon vanilla extract
- Zest of 1 lemon
- 1 cup fresh or frozen blueberries

Air Fryer Machine Settings:

- Preheat your air fryer to 350°F (175°C).

Time:

- Air-fry muffins for 12-15 minutes, until a toothpick inserted comes out clean.

CHAPTER 40
CAJUN SHRIMP TACOS

Bring the bold flavors of Cajun cuisine to your table with Cajun Shrimp Tacos. Learn to season shrimp with a zesty Cajun spice blend, air-fry them to perfection, and assemble delicious tacos with fresh toppings.

Ingredients:

- 1 pound large shrimp, peeled and deveined
- 2 tablespoons Cajun seasoning
- 1 tablespoon olive oil
- Corn or flour tortillas
- Shredded lettuce, diced tomatoes, avocado slices, and cilantro for toppings
- Lime wedges, for serving

Air Fryer Machine Settings:

- Preheat your air fryer to 400°F (200°C).

Time:

- Air-fry shrimp for 6-8 minutes, until they are opaque and slightly crispy.

CHAPTER 41
CRISPY ZUCCHINI PARMESAN CHIPS

Indulge in a healthier twist on a classic with Crispy Zucchini Parmesan Chips. Learn to coat zucchini slices with a flavorful Parmesan and breadcrumb mixture, air-fry to perfection, and enjoy a delightful snack or side dish.

Ingredients:

- 2 medium-sized zucchinis, thinly sliced
- 1 cup breadcrumbs
- 1/2 cup grated Parmesan cheese
- 1 teaspoon garlic powder

- 1 teaspoon dried basil
- 1/2 cup flour
- 2 eggs, beaten
- Marinara sauce, for dipping

Air Fryer Machine Settings:

- Preheat your air fryer to 375°F (190°C).

Time:

- Air-fry zucchini slices for 8-10 minutes, turning halfway, until they are golden brown and crispy.

CHAPTER 42
MEDITERRANEAN QUINOA SALAD WITH LEMON VINAIGRETTE

Savor the freshness of Mediterranean flavors with a Quinoa Salad. Learn to air-fry cherry tomatoes for an added burst of sweetness and create a wholesome salad with quinoa, cucumber, feta, and a zesty lemon vinaigrette.

Ingredients:

- 1 cup quinoa, cooked and cooled
- 1 cup cherry tomatoes
- 1 cucumber, diced
- 1/2 cup Kalamata olives, sliced
- 1/2 cup feta cheese, crumbled
- 1/4 cup red onion, finely chopped
- Fresh parsley, chopped, for garnish

Air Fryer Machine Settings:

- Preheat your air fryer to 375°F (190°C).

Time:

- Air-fry cherry tomatoes for 5-7 minutes, until they are slightly blistered.

CHAPTER 43

SPICED BUTTERNUT SQUASH FRIES

Experience the rich flavors of fall with Spiced Butternut Squash Fries. Learn to season butternut squash strips with a blend of warm spices, air-fry them to a crispy perfection, and enjoy a nutritious and tasty side dish.

Ingredients:

- 1 medium-sized butternut squash, peeled and cut into fries
- 2 tablespoons olive oil
- 1 teaspoon ground cinnamon
- 1/2 teaspoon ground cumin
- 1/2 teaspoon paprika
- Salt and black pepper, to taste
- Maple syrup, for drizzling (optional)

;

Air Fryer Machine Settings:

- Preheat your air fryer to 375°F (190°C).

Time:

- Air-fry butternut squash fries for 15-18 minutes, shaking the basket halfway, until they are golden and tender.

CHAPTER 44
GARLIC BUTTER SHRIMP PASTA

Master the art of creating a quick and delicious meal with Garlic Butter Shrimp Pasta. Learn to air-fry succulent shrimp and toss them with al dente pasta, all coated in a flavorful garlic butter sauce.

Ingredients:

- 1 pound large shrimp, peeled and deveined
- 8 oz linguine or spaghetti
- 4 tablespoons unsalted butter
- 4 cloves garlic, minced
- 1/2 cup chicken broth
- Juice of 1 lemon
- Red pepper flakes, for a hint of spice
- Fresh parsley, chopped, for garnish

Air Fryer Machine Settings:

- Preheat your air fryer to 400°F (200°C).

Time:

- Air-fry shrimp for 6-8 minutes, until they are opaque and slightly crispy.

CHAPTER 45
CARAMELIZED BANANA SUNDAES

Conclude your culinary journey with a sweet treat - Caramelized Banana Sundaes. Learn to air-fry banana slices until caramelized and assemble a delightful sundae with vanilla ice cream, nuts, and a drizzle of c;hocolate sauce.

Ingredients:

- 4 ripe bananas, sliced

- 1/4 cup brown sugar
- 1 teaspoon ground cinnamon
- Vanilla ice cream
- Chopped nuts (almonds, walnuts, or pecans)
- Chocolate sauce, for drizzling

Air Fryer Machine Settings:

- Preheat your air fryer to 375°F (190°C).

Time:

- Air-fry banana slices for 5-7 minutes, until they are caramelized.

CHAPTER 46
PESTO ZOODLES WITH CHERRY TOMATOES

Explore the world of low-carb pasta alternatives with Pesto Zoodles. Learn to spiralize zucchini into noodle-like shapes, air-fry them until just tender, and toss them in a vibrant pesto sauce with burst cherry tomatoes.

Ingredients:

- 4 medium zucchinis, spiralized
- 1 cup cherry tomatoes, halved
- 1/2 cup fresh basil pesto
- 2 tablespoons pine nuts, toasted
- Grated Parmesan cheese, for serving

Air Fryer Machine Settings:

- Preheat your air fryer to 375°F (190°C).

Time:

- Air-fry zoodles for 5-7 minutes, until they are just tender.

CHAPTER 47

RASPBERRY BALSAMIC GLAZED CHICKEN

Elevate your chicken dinner with Raspberry Balsamic Glazed Chicken. Learn to marinate chicken in a sweet and tangy raspberry balsamic sauce, air-fry to perfection, and enjoy a burst of flavors.

Ingredients:

- 4 boneless, skinless chicken breasts
- 1/2 cup fresh raspberries

- 1/4 cup balsamic vinegar
- 2 tablespoons honey
- 1 tablespoon Dijon mustard
- 1 teaspoon thyme, dried
- Salt and black pepper, to taste

Air Fryer Machine Settings:

- Preheat your air fryer to 375°F (190°C).

Time:

- Air-fry chicken breasts for 18-20 minutes, until they are cooked through.

CHAPTER 48

BUFFALO CAULIFLOWER TACOS

Embrace the spicy goodness with Buffalo Cauliflower Tacos. Learn to coat cauliflower florets in a buffalo sauce, air-fry them to a crispy perfection, and assemble flavorful tacos with your favorite toppings.

Ingredients:

- 1 medium cauliflower, cut into florets
- 1/2 cup buffalo sauce
- 1 tablespoon olive oil
- 1 teaspoon garlic powder
- 1 teaspoon onion powder
- Corn or flour tortillas
- Shredded lettuce, diced tomatoes, and ranch dressing for toppings

Air Fryer Machine Settings:

- Preheat your air fryer to 375°F (190°C).

Time:

- Air-fry cauliflower for 15-18 minutes, shaking the basket halfway, until they are crispy.

CHAPTER 49

CAPRESE STUFFED CHICKEN BREAST

Delight your taste buds with Caprese Stuffed Chicken Breast. Learn to butterfly-cut chicken breasts, stuff them with fresh tomatoes, mozzarella, and basil, air-fry until golden, and enjoy a Mediterranean-inspired dish.

Ingredients:

- 4 boneless, skinless chicken breasts

- 1 cup cherry tomatoes, halved
- 1 cup fresh mozzarella, sliced
- Fresh basil leaves
- 2 tablespoons balsamic glaze
- Salt and black pepper, to taste

Air Fryer Machine Settings:

- Preheat your air fryer to 375°F (190°C).

Time:

- Air-fry chicken breasts for 18-20 minutes, until they are cooked through.

CHAPTER 50

APPLE CINNAMON OATMEAL COOKIES

End your culinary journey on a sweet note with

Apple Cinnamon Oatmeal Cookies. Learn to create soft and chewy cookies with the warmth of cinnamon and the sweetness of apples, all air-fried for a quick dessert.

Ingredients:

- 1 cup rolled oats
- 1 cup all-purpose flour
- 1/2 cup unsalted butter, softened
- 1/2 cup brown sugar
- 1/4 cup granulated sugar
- 1 large egg
- 1 teaspoon vanilla extract
- 1 teaspoon ground cinnamon
- 1 cup finely diced apples

Air Fryer Machine Settings:

- Preheat your air fryer to 350°F (175°C).

Time:

- Air-fry cookies for 8-10 minutes, until they are golden brown.

CHAPTER 51

MEDITERRANEAN STUFFED BELL PEPPERS

Take a journey to the Mediterranean with Stuffed Bell Peppers. Learn to fill bell peppers with a mixture of quinoa, chickpeas, olives, and feta cheese, air-fry until the peppers are tender, and enjoy a flavorful and nutritious meal.

Ingredients:

- 4 bell peppers, halved and seeds removed
- 1 cup cooked quinoa
- 1 can (15 oz) chickpeas, drained and rinsed
- 1/2 cup Kalamata olives, chopped
- 1/2 cup feta cheese, crumbled
- 1 cup cherry tomatoes, diced
- 1 teaspoon dried oregano
- 1 teaspoon garlic powder
- Olive oil, for drizzling

Air Fryer Machine Settings:

- Preheat your air fryer to 375°F (190°C).

Time:

- Air-fry stuffed peppers for 20-25 minutes, until they are cooked through and the tops are slightly crispy.

CHAPTER 52

SPINACH AND MUSHROOM QUESADILLAS

Master the art of quick and savory quesadillas with Spinach and Mushroom Quesadillas. Learn to sauté spinach and mushrooms, sandwich them between tortillas with cheese, and air-fry for a crispy exterior and gooey interior.

Ingredients:

- 8 small flour tortillas
- 2 cups fresh spinach
- 1 cup mushrooms, sliced
- 1 cup shredded Monterey Jack cheese
- 1 teaspoon cumin
- 1 teaspoon chili powder
- Sour cream and salsa, for serving

Air Fryer Machine Settings:

- Preheat your air fryer to 375°F (190°C).

Time:

- Air-fry quesadillas for 4-6 minutes, flipping halfway through, until they are golden and cheese is melted.

CHAPTER 53

TERIYAKI PINEAPPLE CHICKEN SKEWERS

Transport your taste buds to the tropics with

Teriyaki Pineapple Chicken Skewers. Learn to marinate chicken in a teriyaki glaze, skewer with pineapple chunks, and air-fry for a deliciously sweet and savory dish.

Ingredients:

- 1.5 pounds chicken breast, cut into cubes
- 1 cup pineapple chunks
- 1/2 cup teriyaki sauce
- 2 tablespoons soy sauce
- 1 tablespoon honey
- 1 tablespoon sesame oil
- Wooden skewers, soaked in water

Air Fryer Machine Settings:

- Preheat your air fryer to 375°F (190°C).

Time:

- Air-fry skewers for 15-18 minutes, turning halfway through, until the chicken is cooked through.

CHAPTER 54

LEMON DILL ROASTED BRUSSELS SPROUTS

Elevate the humble Brussels sprouts with Lemon Dill Roasted Brussels Sprouts. Learn to coat them in a zesty lemon-dill marinade, air-fry until crispy, and enjoy a side dish bursting with flavor.

Ingredients:

- 1 pound Brussels sprouts, halved
- 2 tablespoons olive oil
- Zest of 1 lemon
- 2 tablespoons fresh dill, chopped
- Salt and black pepper, to taste

Air Fryer Machine Settings:

- Preheat your air fryer to 375°F (190°C).

Time:

- Air-fry Brussels sprouts for 15-18 minutes, shaking the basket halfway, until they are crispy and golden.

CHAPTER 55

CHOCOLATE COVERED STRAWBERRY EMPANADAS

End your culinary adventure on a sweet note with Chocolate Covered Strawberry Empanadas. Learn to fill empanada dough with fresh strawberries, air-fry until golden, and drizzle with melted chocolate for a delightful dessert.

Ingredients:

- 2 cups fresh strawberries, diced
- 1/4 cup sugar

- 1 tablespoon cornstarch
- 1 package empanada dough (store-bought or homemade)
- 1/2 cup chocolate chips, melted
- Powdered sugar, for dusting

Air Fryer Machine Settings:

- Preheat your air fryer to 375°F (190°C).

Time:

- Air-fry empanadas for 10-12 minutes, until they are golden and the filling is bubbly.

CHAPTER 56

CRISPY PARMESAN ZUCCHINI FRIES

Ditch traditional fries for a healthier alternative with Crispy Parmesan Zucchini Fries. Learn to coat zucchini sticks in a Parmesan and breadcrumb mixture, air-fry until golden and crunchy, and enjoy a guilt-free snack or side dish.

Ingredients:

- 2 medium-sized zucchinis, cut into fries
- 1 cup breadcrumbs
- 1/2 cup grated Parmesan cheese
- 1 teaspoon garlic powder
- 1 teaspoon dried oregano
- 2 eggs, beaten
- Marinara sauce, for dipping

Air Fryer Machine Settings:

- Preheat your air fryer to 375°F (190°C).

Time:

- Air-fry zucchini fries for 10-12 minutes, turning halfway through, until they are golden and crisp.

CHAPTER 57
THAI BASIL CHICKEN LETTUCE WRAPS

Experience the vibrant flavors of Thai cuisine with Basil Chicken Lettuce Wraps. Learn to stir-fry ground chicken with aromatic Thai basil and create a flavorful filling for lettuce wraps, all with the convenience of your air fryer.

Ingredients:

- 1 pound ground chicken
- 2 tablespoons soy sauce
- 1 tablespoon fish sauce
- 1 tablespoon oyster sauce
- 1 tablespoon sugar
- 3 garlic cloves, minced
- 1 cup fresh Thai basil leaves
- Butter lettuce leaves, for wrapping

Air Fryer Machine Settings:

- Preheat your air fryer to 375°F (190°C).

Time:

- Stir-fry chicken in the air fryer for 10-12 minutes until cooked through.
- Add Thai basil and cook for an additional 2 minutes.

CHAPTER 58
CAPRESE AIR-FRIED AVOCADO

Give avocados a delicious twist with Caprese Air-Fried Avocado. Learn to stuff avocado halves with fresh mozzarella, cherry tomatoes, and basil, air-fry until melty and golden, and enjoy a unique and delightful appetizer.

Ingredients:

- 2 avocados, halved and pitted
- 1 cup cherry tomatoes, halved
- 1 cup fresh mozzarella, diced
- Fresh basil leaves, chopped
- Balsamic glaze, for drizzling

Air Fryer Machine Settings:

- Preheat your air fryer to 375°F (190°C).

Time:

- Air-fry avocado halves for 8-10 minutes, until the cheese is melted and the tops are golden.

CHAPTER 59

LEMON BLUEBERRY PANCAKE BITES

Savor breakfast with Lemon Blueberry Pancake Bites. Learn to make mini pancake bites infused with lemon zest and juicy blueberries, all cooked to perfection in your air fryer.

Ingredients:

- 1 cup pancake mix
- 1/2 cup milk
- 1 egg
- Zest of 1 lemon
- 1/2 cup fresh blueberries

- Maple syrup, for drizzling

Air Fryer Machine Settings:

- Preheat your air fryer to 350°F (175°C).

Time:

- Cook pancake bites in the air fryer for 5-7 minutes, until they are golden brown.

CHAPTER 60

BBQ PULLED PORK STUFFED SWEET POTATOES

Enjoy the comforting flavors of BBQ Pulled Pork Stuffed Sweet Potatoes. Learn to slow-cook pork, shred it, mix with barbecue sauce, and stuff it into sweet potatoes, all finished in the air fryer for a delicious and hearty meal.

Ingredients:

- 2 large sweet potatoes
- 1 pound pork shoulder
- 1 cup barbecue sauce
- 1 teaspoon smoked paprika
- 1 teaspoon garlic powder
- Salt and black pepper, to taste
- Green onions, for garnish

Air Fryer Machine Settings:

- Preheat your air fryer to 400°F (200°C).

Time:

- Air-fry stuffed sweet potatoes for 10-12 minutes, until the tops are crispy.

CHAPTER 61
TERIYAKI VEGETABLE STIR-FRY

Explore the world of vegetarian cuisine with Teriyaki Vegetable Stir-Fry. Learn to air-fry a colorful medley of vegetables in a savory teriyaki sauce for a quick and flavorful meal.

Ingredients:

- 2 cups broccoli florets
- 1 bell pepper, thinly sliced
- 1 carrot, julienned
- 1 cup snap peas
- 1/2 cup sliced mushrooms
- 1/4 cup soy sauce
- 2 tablespoons teriyaki sauce
- 1 tablespoon sesame oil
- 1 tablespoon rice vinegar
- 1 tablespoon honey
- Sesame seeds, for garnish

- Green onions, sliced, for garnish

Air Fryer Machine Settings:

- Preheat your air fryer to 375°F (190°C).

Time:

- Air-fry vegetables for 12-15 minutes, shaking the basket halfway through.

CHAPTER 62

BLACKENED SALMON TACOS

Savor the bold flavors of Blackened Salmon Tacos.

Learn to season salmon fillets with a zesty blackening spice mix, air-fry to perfection, and serve in taco shells with refreshing toppings.

Ingredients:

- 4 salmon fillets
- 2 tablespoons blackening spice mix
- 1 tablespoon olive oil
- Corn or flour tortillas
- Shredded cabbage, diced tomatoes, and avocado slices for toppings
- Lime wedges, for serving

Air Fryer Machine Settings:

- Preheat your air fryer to 375°F (190°C).

Time:

- Air-fry salmon for 10-12 minutes, until it flakes easily with a fork.

CHAPTER 63
MEDITERRANEAN EGGPLANT SLICES

Delight in the flavors of the Mediterranean with air-fried Eggplant Slices. Learn to coat eggplant slices in a flavorful herb mixture and air-fry until they are tender and golden brown.

Ingredients:

- 1 large eggplant, sliced into rounds
- 1/4 cup olive oil
- 2 teaspoons dried oregano
- 1 teaspoon garlic powder
- 1 teaspoon smoked paprika
- Salt and black pepper, to taste
- Tzatziki sauce, for dipping

Air Fryer Machine Settings:

- Preheat your air fryer to 375°F (190°C).

Time:

- Air-fry eggplant slices for 10-12 minutes, flipping halfway through, until they are golden and tender.

CHAPTER 64
PESTO MOZZARELLA STUFFED MUSHROOMS

Elevate the classic stuffed mushrooms with Pesto Mozzarella Filling. Learn to mix pesto with mozzarella, stuff into mushroom caps, and air-fry for a delicious appetizer or side dish.

Ingredients:

- 12 large mushrooms, stems removed

- 1/2 cup fresh mozzarella, diced
- 1/4 cup pesto sauce
- 2 tablespoons breadcrumbs
- Fresh basil, for garnish

Air Fryer Machine Settings:

- Preheat your air fryer to 375°F (190°C).

Time:

- Air-fry stuffed mushrooms for 8-10 minutes, until the cheese is melted and the tops are golden.

CHAPTER 65

CINNAMON SUGAR APPLE CHIPS

Indulge in a sweet and healthy snack with Cinnamon Sugar Apple Chips. Learn to thinly slice apples, dust them with cinnamon sugar, and air-fry until they are crispy and irresistible.

Ingredients:

- 3 medium-sized apples, thinly sliced
- 1 tablespoon sugar
- 1 teaspoon ground cinnamon

Air Fryer Machine Settings:

- Preheat your air fryer to 375°F (190°C).

Time:

- Air-fry apple slices for 8-10 minutes, flipping halfway through, until they are golden and crispy.

CHAPTER 66
CAPRESE STUFFED MUSHROOMS

Experience the classic Caprese combination in bite-sized form. Learn to stuff mushrooms with fresh mozzarella, cherry tomatoes, and basil, air-fry until gooey and delightful.

Ingredients:

- 12 large mushrooms, stems removed
- 1 cup cherry tomatoes, halved
- 1 cup fresh mozzarella, diced
- Fresh basil leaves, chopped
- Balsamic glaze, for drizzling

Air Fryer Machine Settings:

- Preheat your air fryer to 375°F (190°C).

Time:

- Air-fry stuffed mushrooms for 8-10 minutes, until the cheese is melted and the tops are golden.

CHAPTER 67

GARLIC ROSEMARY HASSELBACK POTATOES

Master the art of crispy and flavorful Hasselback Potatoes with a garlic and rosemary twist, air-fried to perfection.

Ingredients:

- 4 large russet potatoes, washed
- 4 tablespoons olive oil
- 4 cloves garlic, minced
- 2 tablespoons fresh rosemary, chopped
- Salt and black pepper, to taste

Air Fryer Machine Settings:

- Preheat your air fryer to 400°F (200°C).

Time:

- Air-fry potatoes for 35-40 minutes, flipping halfway through, until they are golden and crispy.

CHAPTER 68
COCONUT LIME SHRIMP SKEWERS

Transport your taste buds to the tropics with Coconut Lime Shrimp Skewers. Learn to marinate shrimp in a coconut-lime mixture, skewer, and air-fry for a quick and flavorful dish.

Ingredients:

- 1 pound large shrimp, peeled and deveined
- 1/2 cup coconut milk
- Zest and juice of 2 limes
- 2 tablespoons soy sauce
- 1 tablespoon honey
- 1 teaspoon ground coriander
- Wooden skewers, soaked in water

Air Fryer Machine Settings:

- Preheat your air fryer to 375°F (190°C).

Time:

- Air-fry skewers for 8-10 minutes, turning halfway through, until shrimp are opaque.

CHAPTER 69

MAPLE DIJON GLAZED BRUSSELS SPROUTS

Elevate Brussels sprouts with a sweet and tangy

Maple Dijon Glaze, air-fried until they are crispy on the outside and tender on the inside.

Ingredients:

- 1 pound Brussels sprouts, halved
- 2 tablespoons olive oil
- 2 tablespoons maple syrup

- 1 tablespoon Dijon mustard
- Salt and black pepper, to taste

Air Fryer Machine Settings:

- Preheat your air fryer to 375°F (190°C).

Time:

- Air-fry Brussels sprouts for 15-18 minutes, shaking the basket halfway, until they are crispy.

CHAPTER 70
LEMON GARLIC SHRIMP PASTA

Indulge in a quick and flavorful Lemon Garlic Shrimp Pasta. Learn to air-fry shrimp and toss them with al dente pasta, all coated in a zesty lemon garlic sauce.

Ingredients:

- 1 pound large shrimp, peeled and deveined
- 8 oz linguine or spaghetti
- 4 tablespoons unsalted butter
- 4 cloves garlic, minced
- Zest and juice of 1 lemon
- Red pepper flakes, for a hint of spice
- Fresh parsley, chopped, for garnish

Air Fryer Machine Settings:

- Preheat your air fryer to 400°F (200°C).

Time:

- Air-fry shrimp for 6-8 minutes, until they are opaque and slightly crispy.

CHAPTER 71
BALSAMIC GLAZED PORTOBELLO MUSHROOMS

Delight in the rich flavor of Balsamic Glazed Portobello Mushrooms. Learn to marinate and air-fry these mushrooms until they are juicy and infused with tangy balsamic goodness.

Ingredients:

- 4 large Portobello mushrooms, stems removed
- 1/4 cup balsamic vinegar
- 2 tablespoons olive oil
- 2 cloves garlic, minced
- 1 teaspoon dried thyme
- Salt and black pepper, to taste

Air Fryer Machine Settings:

- Preheat your air fryer to 375°F (190°C).

Time:

- Air-fry mushrooms for 12-15 minutes, turning halfway through, until they are tender.

CHAPTER 72
PANKO CRUSTED CHICKEN TENDERS

Master the art of crispy Panko Crusted Chicken Tenders, air-fried to golden perfection. Learn to coat chicken strips in a seasoned panko mixture for a delightful crunch.

Ingredients:

- 1 pound chicken tenders
- 1 cup panko breadcrumbs
- 1/2 cup grated Parmesan cheese

- 1 teaspoon garlic powder
- 1 teaspoon smoked paprika
- 2 eggs, beaten
- Marinara or honey mustard, for dipping

Air Fryer Machine Settings:

- Preheat your air fryer to 375°F (190°C).

Time:

- Air-fry chicken tenders for 12-15 minutes, turning halfway through, until they are golden and crispy.

CHAPTER 73

CHILI LIME CORN ON THE COB

Spice up your corn on the cob with Chili Lime seasoning, air-fried for a flavorful and zesty twist on a classic side dish.

Ingredients:

- 4 ears of corn, husked and halved
- 2 tablespoons melted butter
- 1 teaspoon chili powder
- Zest and juice of 1 lime
- Salt, to taste
- Fresh cilantro, chopped, for garnish

Air Fryer Machine Settings:

- ✓ Preheat your air fryer to 400°F (200°C).

Time:

- ✓ Air-fry corn for 12-15 minutes, turning halfway through, until it's cooked and slightly charred.

CHAPTER 74
SOUTHWEST STUFFED BELL PEPPERS

Enjoy a flavorful and satisfying meal with Southwest Stuffed Bell Peppers. Learn to fill bell peppers with a mixture of seasoned ground turkey, black beans, corn, and cheese, air-fried to perfection.

Ingredients:

- 4 bell peppers, halved and seeds removed
- 1 pound ground turkey
- 1 cup black beans, cooked
- 1 cup corn kernels
- 1 cup shredded cheddar cheese

- 1 teaspoon cumin
- 1 teaspoon chili powder
- Salt and black pepper, to taste

Air Fryer Machine Settings:

- ✓ Preheat your air fryer to 375°F (190°C).

Time:

- ✓ Air-fry stuffed peppers for 20-25 minutes, until they are cooked through and the tops are slightly crispy.

CHAPTER 75

SPINACH AND FETA STUFFED CHICKEN BREASTS

Delight in Spinach and Feta Stuffed Chicken Breasts, air-fried until the chicken is juicy and the filling is melty and flavorful.

Ingredients:

- 4 boneless, skinless chicken breasts
- 2 cups fresh spinach, chopped
- 1 cup feta cheese, crumbled
- 2 cloves garlic, minced
- 1 teaspoon dried oregano
- Salt and black pepper, to taste
- Olive oil, for brushing

Air Fryer Machine Settings:

- ✓ Preheat your air fryer to 375°F (190°C).

Time:

- ✓ Air-fry chicken breasts for 18-20 minutes, until they are cooked through.

CHAPTER 76
LEMON HERB QUINOA SALAD

Create a refreshing and nutrient-packed Lemon Herb Quinoa Salad. Learn to air-fry quinoa until it's crispy and golden, then toss it with fresh herbs, veggies, and a zesty lemon dressing.

Ingredients:

- 1 cup quinoa, cooked
- 1 cup cherry tomatoes, halved
- 1 cucumber, diced

- 1/2 cup Kalamata olives, chopped
- 1/4 cup feta cheese, crumbled
- Fresh parsley, chopped
- Zest and juice of 1 lemon
- 3 tablespoons olive oil
- Salt and black pepper, to taste

Air Fryer Machine Settings:

- ✓ Preheat your air fryer to 375°F (190°C).

Time:

- ✓ Air-fry cooked quinoa for 8-10 minutes, shaking the basket occasionally, until it's crispy.

CHAPTER 77

HONEY SRIRACHA GLAZED CHICKEN WINGS

Indulge in the perfect combination of sweet and spicy with Honey Sriracha Glazed Chicken Wings, air-fried to achieve a crispy and sticky exterior.

Ingredients:

- 2 pounds chicken wings, split at joints, tips discarded
- 1/4 cup honey
- 2 tablespoons Sriracha sauce
- 2 tablespoons soy sauce
- 1 tablespoon sesame oil
- 1 tablespoon rice vinegar
- Sesame seeds and green onions, for garnish

Air Fryer Machine Settings:

- ✓ Preheat your air fryer to 400°F (200°C).

Time:

- ✓ Air-fry chicken wings for 25-30 minutes, turning halfway through, until they are crispy and glazed.

CHAPTER 78

BLUEBERRY BALSAMIC GLAZED SALMON

Delight in the sweet and tangy combination of Blueberry Balsamic Glazed Salmon, air-fried for a quick and elegant dinner option.

Ingredients:

- 4 salmon fillets

- 1 cup fresh blueberries
- 1/4 cup balsamic vinegar
- 2 tablespoons honey
- 1 tablespoon olive oil
- 1 teaspoon thyme, dried
- Salt and black pepper, to taste

Air Fryer Machine Settings:

✓ Preheat your air fryer to 375°F (190°C).

Time:

✓ Air-fry salmon fillets for 10-12 minutes, until they are cooked through.

CHAPTER 79
CAJUN SHRIMP AND SAUSAGE SKEWERS

Savor the bold flavors of Cajun cuisine with Shrimp and Sausage Skewers. Learn to season shrimp and sausage with Cajun spices, skewer, and air-fry for a tasty dish.

Ingredients:

- 1 pound large shrimp, peeled and deveined
- 1/2 pound Andouille sausage, sliced
- 1 tablespoon Cajun seasoning
- 2 tablespoons olive oil
- Wooden skewers, soaked in water

Air Fryer Machine Settings:

- ✓ Preheat your air fryer to 375°F (190°C).

Time:

- ✓ Air-fry skewers for 8-10 minutes, turning halfway through, until shrimp are opaque.

CHAPTER 81

SPINACH AND ARTICHOKE STUFFED CHICKEN

Transform chicken breasts into a gourmet dish with a creamy spinach and artichoke filling. Air-fry until golden brown for a delectable and elegant entrée.

Ingredients:

- 4 boneless, skinless chicken breasts
- 1 cup frozen chopped spinach, thawed and drained
- 1 cup canned artichoke hearts, chopped

- 1/2 cup cream cheese
- 1/4 cup grated Parmesan cheese
- 2 cloves garlic, minced
- Salt and black pepper, to taste

Air Fryer Machine Settings:

✓ Preheat your air fryer to 375°F (190°C).

Time:

✓ Air-fry stuffed chicken breasts for 18-20 minutes or until the internal temperature reaches 165°F (74°C).

CHAPTER 82

SWEET AND SPICY PINEAPPLE SHRIMP SKEWERS

Transport your taste buds to the tropics with these Sweet and Spicy Pineapple Shrimp Skewers. Marinate shrimp in a delightful sweet and spicy sauce, skewer with pineapple chunks, and air-fry for a quick and flavorful seafood dish.

Ingredients:

- 1 pound large shrimp, peeled and deveined
- 1 cup pineapple chunks
- 1/4 cup honey
- 2 tablespoons soy sauce
- 1 tablespoon Sriracha
- 1 tablespoon lime juice
- Wooden skewers, soaked in water

Air Fryer Machine Settings:

- ✓ Preheat your air fryer to 375°F (190°C).

Time:

- ✓ Air-fry shrimp skewers for 10-12 minutes, turning halfway through.

CHAPTER 83

COCONUT LIME CHICKEN TENDERS

Add a tropical twist to classic chicken tenders with Coconut Lime Chicken Tenders. Coated in a crispy coconut crust and infused with zesty lime flavor, these tenders are a delightful and refreshing treat.

Ingredients:

- 1 pound chicken tenders

- 1 cup shredded coconut
- 1/2 cup breadcrumbs
- Zest of 2 limes
- 1/4 cup lime juice
- 2 eggs, beaten
- Salt and black pepper, to taste

Air Fryer Machine Settings:

- ✓ Preheat your air fryer to 375°F (190°C).

Time:

- ✓ Air-fry chicken tenders for 12-15 minutes, turning halfway, until they are golden and crispy.

CHAPTER 84
HERB-MARINATED LAMB CHOPS

Elevate your dinner with Herb-Marinated Lamb Chops. Marinate lamb chops in a blend of fresh herbs, air-fry to perfection, and serve with a side of mint sauce for a gourmet meal.

Ingredients:

- 8 lamb chops
- 1/4 cup olive oil
- 2 tablespoons fresh rosemary, chopped
- 2 tablespoons fresh thyme, chopped
- 2 cloves garlic, minced
- Salt and black pepper, to taste

Air Fryer Machine Settings:

- ✓ Preheat your air fryer to 375°F (190°C).

Time:

- ✓ Air-fry lamb chops for 10-12 minutes for medium-rare, adjusting time for desired doneness.

CHAPTER 85

RASPBERRY ALMOND MINI CHEESECAKES

Indulge your sweet tooth with these Raspberry Almond Mini Cheesecakes. Air-fry individual-sized cheesecakes with a raspberry swirl and almond crust for a delightful dessert.

Ingredients:

- 8 oz cream cheese, softened
- 1/2 cup granulated sugar

- 1/2 cup sour cream
- 2 large eggs
- 1 teaspoon almond extract
- 1/2 cup raspberry jam
- 1 cup graham cracker crumbs
- 2 tablespoons unsalted butter, melted

Air Fryer Machine Settings:

- ✓ Preheat your air fryer to 325°F (163°C).

Time:

- ✓ Air-fry mini cheesecakes for 12-15 minutes, until the centers are set.

CHAPTER 86
BBQ PULLED CHICKEN SLIDERS

Create savory and satisfying BBQ Pulled Chicken Sliders with the convenience of your air fryer. Slow-cook chicken, shred it, mix with barbecue sauce, and serve on slider buns for a crowd-pleasing appetizer or meal.

Ingredients:

- 2 pounds boneless, skinless chicken breasts
- 1 cup barbecue sauce
- 1 teaspoon smoked paprika
- 1 teaspoon garlic powder
- Salt and black pepper, to taste
- Slider buns
- Coleslaw, for topping (optional)

Air Fryer Machine Settings:

- ✓ Preheat your air fryer to 375°F (190°C).

Time:

- ✓ Air-fry pulled chicken for 10-12 minutes, stirring occasionally.

CHAPTER 87
LEMON POPPY SEED DONUTS

Satisfy your sweet cravings with these Air-Fried Lemon Poppy Seed Donuts. Infused with zesty lemon flavor and studded with poppy seeds, these donuts are a delightful treat.

Ingredients:

- 1 cup all-purpose flour
- 1/2 cup granulated sugar

- 1 teaspoon baking powder
- 1/4 teaspoon baking soda
- 1/4 teaspoon salt
- 1/4 cup unsalted butter, melted
- 1/2 cup buttermilk
- 1 large egg
- Zest of 1 lemon
- 1 tablespoon poppy seeds
- Powdered sugar, for dusting

Air Fryer Machine Settings:

- ✓ Preheat your air fryer to 350°F (175°C).

Time:

- ✓ Air-fry donuts for 8-10 minutes, until they are golden brown.

CHAPTER 88

BUFFALO CHICKEN MEATBALLS

Turn up the heat with Buffalo Chicken Meatballs.

Air-fry these spicy and flavorful meatballs, then toss them in buffalo sauce for a crowd-pleasing appetizer or a zesty main dish.

Ingredients:

- 1 pound ground chicken
- 1/2 cup breadcrumbs
- 1/4 cup grated Parmesan cheese
- 1/4 cup chopped green onions
- 1/4 cup hot sauce
- 2 tablespoons melted butter
- 1 large egg
- Celery sticks and blue cheese dressing, for serving

Air Fryer Machine Settings:

- ✓ Preheat your air fryer to 375°F (190°C).

Time:

- ✓ Air-fry meatballs for 12-15 minutes, turning halfway through, until they are cooked through.

CHAPTER 89
CILANTRO LIME SHRIMP TACOS

Bring a burst of freshness to your table with Cilantro Lime Shrimp Tacos. Marinate shrimp in a zesty cilantro lime mixture, air-fry to perfection, and serve in soft taco shells with your favorite toppings.

Ingredients:

- 1 pound large shrimp, peeled and deveined
- 1/4 cup fresh cilantro, chopped

- 2 tablespoons lime juice
- 1 tablespoon olive oil
- 1 teaspoon cumin
- 1 teaspoon chili powder
- Salt and black pepper, to taste
- Corn or flour tortillas
- Shredded cabbage, diced tomatoes, and avocado slices for toppings

Air Fryer Machine Settings:

- ✓ Preheat your air fryer to 375°F (190°C).

Time:

- ✓ Air-fry shrimp for 8-10 minutes, until they are cooked through.

CHAPTER 90
CHOCOLATE PEANUT BUTTER BANANA EMPANADAS

Indulge your sweet tooth with Chocolate Peanut Butter Banana Empanadas. Fill empanada dough with a delightful mixture of chocolate, peanut butter, and banana, air-fry until golden, and enjoy a delicious dessert.

Ingredients:

- 2 ripe bananas, mashed
- 1/4 cup peanut butter
- 1/4 cup chocolate chips
- 1 package empanada dough (store-bought or homemade)
- Powdered sugar, for dusting

Air Fryer Machine Settings:

- ✓ Preheat your air fryer to 375°F (190°C).

Time:

- ✓ Air-fry empanadas for 10-12 minutes, until they are golden and the filling is bubbly.

CHAPTER 91

GREEK CHICKEN SOUVLAKI SKEWERS

Take your taste buds to Greece with Greek Chicken Souvlaki Skewers. Marinate chicken in Mediterranean flavors, skewer, and air-fry for a delicious and satisfying dish.

Ingredients:

- 1.5 pounds chicken breast, cut into cubes
- 1/4 cup olive oil

- 2 tablespoons red wine vinegar
- 1 tablespoon dried oregano
- 1 teaspoon garlic powder
- Salt and black pepper, to taste
- Tzatziki sauce, for dipping

Air Fryer Machine Settings:

- ✓ Preheat your air fryer to 375°F (190°C).

Time:

- ✓ Air-fry skewers for 15-18 minutes, turning halfway through, until the chicken is cooked through.

CHAPTER 92
RASPBERRY CHOCOLATE CHIP PANCAKES

Start your day with a delightful breakfast of Raspberry Chocolate Chip Pancakes. Mix raspberries and chocolate chips into pancake batter, air-fry until fluffy, and enjoy a sweet and fruity morning treat.

Ingredients:

- 1 cup pancake mix
- 1/2 cup milk
- 1 egg
- 1/2 cup fresh raspberries
- 1/4 cup chocolate chips

Air Fryer Machine Settings:

- ✓ Preheat your air fryer to 350°F (175°C).

Time:

- ✓ Cook pancakes in the air fryer for 5-7 minutes, until they are golden brown.

CHAPTER 93
GARLIC BUTTER STEAK BITES

Savor the rich flavors of Garlic Butter Steak Bites.

Season steak bites, cook them to perfection in the air fryer, and toss in a garlic butter sauce for a mouthwatering dish.

Ingredients:

- 1 pound sirloin or ribeye steak, cut into bite-sized pieces
- 2 tablespoons olive oil
- 4 cloves garlic, minced
- 2 tablespoons butter

- Fresh parsley, chopped, for garnish

Air Fryer Machine Settings:

- ✓ Preheat your air fryer to 400°F (200°C).

Time:

- ✓ Air-fry steak bites for 8-10 minutes for medium-rare, adjusting time for desired doneness.

PHASE II

INTRODUCTION TO AIR FRYING

Welcome to "Air Fryer Recipe Instructor: The Art and Science of Air Frying," where we embark on a culinary journey into the fascinating world of air frying. In this introductory chapter, we delve into the roots and evolution of air frying technology, uncovering the secrets that make this method of cooking both an art and a science.

BRIEF HISTORY AND EVOLUTION OF AIR FRYING TECHNOLOGY

The concept of air frying traces its roots back to the early 20th century, but it wasn't until recent years that it gained widespread popularity. We explore the innovative minds and technological advancements that paved the way for the creation of the modern air fryer. From the initial experiments with convection ovens to the development of specialized air frying appliances, we witness the evolution of a cooking technique that has transformed the way we approach our favorite dishes.

Discover the pioneers who envisioned a healthier and more efficient way to achieve the crispiness of deep frying without the excessive use of oil. Learn how the marriage of convection, radiant heat, and rapid air circulation culminated in the birth of the air fryer as we know it today.

OVERVIEW OF THE BENEFITS OF AIR FRYING COMPARED TO TRADITIONAL COOKING METHODS

As we embark on this culinary adventure, it's essential to understand why air frying has captured the imaginations of home cooks and professional chefs alike. We'll explore the myriad benefits that set air frying apart from traditional cooking methods.

Say goodbye to the guilt associated with indulging in your favorite fried foods. With significantly less oil, air frying offers a healthier alternative without compromising on flavor and texture. We'll delve into the science behind this, examining how the rapid circulation of hot air creates the perfect environment for achieving that coveted crispy exterior while maintaining the juiciness of the interior.

Beyond health, we'll discuss the time-saving advantages of air frying. No more waiting for the oven to preheat or oil to reach the right temperature. The air fryer's quick start-up and cooking times make it a practical choice for busy individuals and families.

Join us as we unlock the secrets of air frying, blending the artistry of culinary innovation with the precision of scientific principles. "Air Fryer Recipe Instructor" is not just a cookbook; it's a guide to mastering the art and science of air frying for a delicious and wholesome culinary experience.

CHAPTER 1
CHOOSING THE RIGHT AIR FRYER

Welcome to the first chapter of "Air Fryer Recipe Instructor: The Art and Science of Air Frying." In this crucial chapter, we embark on the journey of selecting the perfect air fryer, a decision that sets the stage for your culinary adventures. Let's navigate through the diverse landscape of air fryers and explore the factors that will guide you in making the best choice for your kitchen.

TYPES OF AIR FRYERS AVAILABLE IN THE MARKET

The market offers a variety of air fryers, each designed with unique features to cater to different preferences and cooking needs. We'll unravel the distinctions among the main types:

1. **Basket-style Air Fryers:**
   ✓ Explore the classic design with a removable basket, making it easy to shake and toss ingredients during cooking.
   ✓ Ideal for those who enjoy the familiarity of a traditional frying experience.

2. **Oven-style Air Fryers:**
   ✓ Delve into the versatility of air frying in an oven-like setting, suitable for larger batches and accommodating various cooking accessories.
   ✓ Discover how these models often offer additional functions beyond air frying.

3. **Toaster Oven Air Fryers:**
   ✓ Combine the convenience of a toaster oven with the air frying capability, saving counter space and simplifying meal preparation.
   ✓ Ideal for those with limited kitchen real estate.

4. **Oil-less Fryers:**

- ✓ Explore innovative technologies that use minimal or no oil, focusing on hot air circulation to achieve a crispy finish.
- ✓ Uncover the health-conscious options available in the market.

Understanding these types provides the foundation for finding an air fryer that aligns with your cooking style, kitchen space, and culinary aspirations.

FACTORS TO CONSIDER WHEN SELECTING THE BEST AIR FRYER FOR YOUR NEEDS

Now that we've identified the different types of air fryers, let's delve into the key factors that will help you make an informed decision:

1. **Capacity:**
   - ✓ Assess your typical meal size and the number of people you'll be cooking for. Choose an air fryer

with an appropriate capacity to meet your needs without compromising efficiency.

2. **Power and Wattage:**
   ✓ Explore the power and wattage specifications to understand the cooking speed and efficiency. Higher wattage often means faster cooking times.

3. **Controls and Settings:**
   ✓ Evaluate the user interface and controls. Consider your comfort level with programmable options, pre-set modes, and ease of operation.

4. **Size and Design:**
   ✓ Take into account the available space in your kitchen. Opt for a size and design that seamlessly integrates with your kitchen layout and complements your aesthetic preferences.

5. **Cleaning and Maintenance:**

✓ Consider the ease of cleaning, including dishwasher-safe components and accessibility for routine maintenance.

Armed with this knowledge, you're ready to embark on the exciting journey of choosing an air fryer that aligns with your culinary ambitions. Join us as we continue to explore the art and science of air frying in the chapters that follow.

CHAPTER 2

UNDERSTANDING HOW AIR FRYERS WORK**

Welcome to the heart of "Air Fryer Recipe Instructor: The Art and Science of Air Frying." In this chapter, we'll unravel the mystery behind the magic – the science that makes air frying not just a cooking method but a culinary revelation. Join us as we explore the intricate workings of air fryers and the fascinating technologies that drive them.

THE SCIENCE BEHIND AIR FRYING AND ITS COOKING MECHANISM

At its core, air frying is a culinary marvel that combines the principles of convection and rapid air technology. Let's delve into the science that transforms hot air into a culinary powerhouse:

1. Convection Cooking:
- ✓ Uncover the magic of convection, where hot air circulates around the food, creating an environment of consistent heat.
- ✓ Explore how this even heat distribution results in uniform cooking, ensuring every inch of your dish is perfectly cooked.

2. Maillard Reaction:
- ✓ Delve into the Maillard reaction, the chemical process responsible for the browning and development of complex flavors in your favorite dishes.
- ✓ Understand how air frying harnesses this reaction to create that irresistible crispy texture on the outside while maintaining juiciness inside.

3. Reduced Moisture:
- ✓ Examine how the air fryer's rapid air circulation reduces moisture on the food's surface,

contributing to the desired crispiness without excessive oil.

4. High-Heat Environment:
✓ Learn how air fryers generate a high-heat environment quickly, shortening cooking times and preserving the nutritional value of ingredients.

EXPLAINING CONVECTION AND RAPID AIR TECHNOLOGY

1. Convection Technology:
✓ Demystify the concept of convection and how it differs from traditional ovens and cooking methods.
✓ Understand how the fan-driven circulation of hot air enhances cooking efficiency and promotes a healthier approach to frying.

2. Rapid Air Technology:

- ✓ Explore the cutting-edge innovation of rapid air technology, the driving force behind the quick and efficient cooking process in air fryers.
- ✓ Uncover how this technology not only reduces cooking times but also ensures a more energy-efficient and eco-friendly cooking experience.

Understanding these scientific principles empowers you to make the most of your air fryer, transforming everyday ingredients into culinary masterpieces. As we progress through "Air Fryer Recipe Instructor," you'll apply this knowledge to craft delectable dishes that perfectly marry the art and science of air frying. Get ready to elevate your culinary skills to new heights!

CHAPTER 3

ESSENTIAL TOOLS AND ACCESSORIES

Welcome to the practical realm of "Air Fryer Recipe Instructor: The Art and Science of Air Frying." In this chapter, we'll explore the indispensable tools and accessories that will elevate your air frying experience to new heights. Additionally, we'll delve into essential tips on maintaining and cleaning your air fryer, ensuring its longevity and peak performance.

MUST-HAVE TOOLS AND ACCESSORIES FOR EFFICIENT AIR FRYING

1. **Oil Sprayer:**
   - ✓ Discover the importance of an oil sprayer for applying a fine mist of oil to achieve that perfect crispiness without excess oil.
   - ✓ Learn how to choose the right oil and maintain your sprayer for consistent results.

2. Cooking Racks and Skewers:
- ✓ Explore the versatility of cooking racks and skewers for maximizing your air fryer's cooking capacity.
- ✓ Uncover innovative ways to layer ingredients for efficient and even cooking.

3. Parchment Paper and Liners:
- ✓ Understand how parchment paper and liners can simplify cleanup and prevent sticking.
- ✓ Discover creative uses for parchment paper to enhance your air-fried creations.

4. Meat Thermometer:
- ✓ Embrace the precision of a meat thermometer to ensure your meats are perfectly cooked every time.
- ✓ Learn the ideal internal temperatures for various meats and poultry.

5. **Silicone Tongs and Basting Brush:**
   ✓ Master the art of flipping and turning with silicone-tipped tongs, ensuring delicate items remain intact.
   ✓ Explore the benefits of a basting brush for adding layers of flavor without excess oil.

6. **Air Fryer-Specific Cookware:**
   ✓ Consider specialized accessories like baking pans, pizza stones, and silicone molds designed for air fryer use.
   ✓ Experiment with these tools to expand your repertoire beyond traditional air frying.

TIPS ON MAINTAINING AND CLEANING YOUR AIR FRYER

1. **Regular Cleaning Routine:**
   ✓ Establish a simple and effective cleaning routine to maintain the cleanliness of your air fryer after each use.

- ✓ Explore tips on cleaning the basket, tray, and other removable components.

2. **Dealing with Residue and Stains:**
- ✓ Learn how to tackle stubborn residue and stains using gentle cleaning solutions.
- ✓ Understand the importance of avoiding harsh chemicals that could damage your air fryer.

3. **Deep Cleaning Techniques:**
- ✓ Explore step-by-step instructions for deep cleaning your air fryer at regular intervals.
- ✓ Ensure the longevity and optimal performance of your appliance by removing accumulated grease and debris.

4. **Storage and Maintenance:**
- ✓ Receive guidance on proper storage to prevent damage and ensure your air fryer is ready for use whenever inspiration strikes.

✓ Understand maintenance tips for preserving the longevity of your air fryer.

Armed with these essential tools, accessories, and maintenance tips, you're well-equipped to embark on your air frying journey with confidence. Join us as we continue to unravel the secrets of "Air Fryer Recipe Instructor" in the chapters that follow.

CHAPTER 4

MASTERING AIR FRYER CONTROLS

Welcome to a pivotal chapter of "Air Fryer Recipe Instructor: The Art and Science of Air Frying." In this section, we'll delve into the intricate world of air fryer controls, unraveling the diverse settings and functionalities that empower you to orchestrate culinary symphonies with precision. Additionally, we'll equip you with the knowledge to troubleshoot common issues, ensuring smooth operations every time you engage your air fryer.

A DETAILED GUIDE TO THE VARIOUS SETTINGS AND CONTROLS ON AN AIR FRYER

1. **Temperature Control:**
   - ✓ Understand the significance of temperature settings and how they impact cooking outcomes.
   - ✓ Learn the optimal temperatures for different types of dishes, from crispy appetizers to succulent main courses.

2. **Time Settings:**
   - ✓ Delve into the intricacies of time settings, mastering the art of precise cooking durations.
   - ✓ Explore how timing contributes to achieving the perfect balance between crispiness and tenderness.

3. **Preheat Function:**
   ✓ Grasp the importance of preheating and how it enhances the overall cooking process.
   ✓ Learn when to use the preheat function for optimal results.

4. **Programmed Modes:**
   ✓ Navigate through pre-programmed modes for specific dishes, such as fries, chicken, or desserts.
   ✓ Unlock the convenience of one-touch cooking tailored to your favorite recipes.

5. **Pause and Resume Feature:**
   ✓ Explore the benefits of the pause and resume feature, allowing you to check or adjust your creations mid-cooking.
   ✓ Learn how to make the most of this functionality for customized results.

6. **Shut-off and Keep Warm Functions:**
   ✓ Understand automatic shut-off and keep warm functions, enhancing safety and maintaining food temperature.
   ✓ Discover scenarios where these functions prove invaluable in your air frying endeavors.

TROUBLESHOOTING COMMON ISSUES WITH AIR FRYER OPERATION

1. **Uneven Cooking:**
   ✓ Identify potential causes of uneven cooking and explore strategies to achieve uniform results.
   ✓ Learn how to rotate and arrange food for optimal air circulation.

2. **Smoke or Unpleasant Odors:**
   ✓ Address issues related to smoke or odors, ensuring a pleasant cooking environment.
   ✓ Discover tips on preventing and mitigating these concerns.

3. Excessive Noise:
- ✓ Troubleshoot excessive noise during operation and identify potential solutions.
- ✓ Understand when certain sounds are normal and when they may indicate an issue.

4. Inaccurate Temperature or Timer Readings:
- ✓ Explore steps to address discrepancies in temperature or timer readings.
- ✓ Ensure the accuracy of your air fryer settings for consistent results.

5. Malfunctions and Error Codes:
- ✓ Decipher common error codes and troubleshoot malfunctions effectively.
- ✓ Understand when it's appropriate to seek professional assistance for more complex issues.

CHAPTER 5

PREPPING INGREDIENTS FOR AIR FRYING

Welcome to a crucial chapter in "Air Fryer Recipe Instructor: The Art and Science of Air Frying." In this section, we'll dive into the essential steps of preparing your ingredients—a pivotal process that lays the foundation for achieving optimal results in your air fryer. Additionally, we'll explore the art of marinating and seasoning, unlocking the secrets to infusing your creations with flavors that captivate the senses.

PROPERLY PREPARING INGREDIENTS FOR OPTIMAL AIR FRYING RESULTS

1. **Drying Ingredients:**
   - ✓ Understand the importance of patting ingredients dry before air frying.

✓ Explore how moisture affects the crispiness of the final result and how to mitigate excess moisture.

2. **Uniform Sizing:**
   ✓ Master the art of cutting ingredients into uniform sizes for consistent cooking.
   ✓ Learn how size consistency contributes to achieving the perfect balance between crispiness and tenderness.

3. **Coating for Crispiness:**
   ✓ Explore coating options such as breadcrumbs, panko, or a light batter to enhance crispiness.
   ✓ Understand the science behind coatings and how they interact with the air frying process.

4. **Layering Techniques:**
   ✓ Discover effective layering techniques to maximize air circulation.

✓ Learn when and how to layer ingredients for efficient and even cooking.

5. **Thawing Frozen Ingredients:**
   ✓ Navigate the process of thawing frozen ingredients before air frying.
   ✓ Uncover tips to prevent excess moisture accumulation during the thawing process.

TIPS ON MARINATING AND SEASONING FOR ENHANCED FLAVORS

1. **Balancing Flavors:**
   ✓ Explore the art of balancing flavors in your marinades and seasonings.
   ✓ Understand how sweetness, acidity, saltiness, and umami contribute to a harmonious taste profile.

2. **Marinating Times:**

- ✓ Learn the optimal marinating times for different types of proteins and vegetables.
- ✓ Understand the science behind marinating and its impact on flavor absorption.

3. Dry Rubs and Seasoning Blends:
- ✓ Experiment with dry rubs and seasoning blends to add depth and complexity to your dishes.
- ✓ Discover how to create your signature blends that complement the natural flavors of the ingredients.

4. Infusing Aromatics:
- ✓ Embrace the aromatic power of herbs, spices, and aromatics in your air-fried creations.
- ✓ Explore creative ways to infuse your dishes with enticing scents that enhance the overall experience.

5. Oil Infusions:

- ✓ Understand the role of infused oils in elevating the flavor profile of your air-fried dishes.
- ✓ Experiment with different infused oil combinations to tailor your creations to your taste preferences.

As you master the art of preparing ingredients for air frying, you'll unlock the full potential of your culinary creations. Join us in the following chapters of "Air Fryer Recipe Instructor" as we continue to explore the intricacies of air frying, blending science with creativity for a truly transformative cooking experience.

CHAPTER 6
APPETIZERS AND SNACKS

Welcome to the delightful world of "Air Fryer Recipe Instructor: The Art and Science of Air Frying." In this chapter, we embark on a culinary adventure dedicated to crafting irresistible appetizers and snacks—a realm where the air fryer truly shines. Join us as we explore a collection of delectable and crispy creations that will elevate your gatherings and satisfy your snack cravings. Additionally, we'll spark your culinary creativity with innovative ideas for unique air-fried starters.

A COLLECTION OF DELICIOUS AND CRISPY APPETIZERS AND SNACKS

1. **Classic Mozzarella Sticks:**
   ✓ Dive into the timeless appeal of golden-brown mozzarella sticks with a perfectly melted interior.

- ✓ Explore variations in coating and dipping sauces to customize this beloved snack.

2. Crispy Chicken Wings:
- ✓ Elevate your wing game with air-fried perfection—crispy on the outside, juicy on the inside.
- ✓ Experiment with an array of marinades and sauces to suit your taste preferences.

3. Zesty Potato Skins:
- ✓ Rediscover the joy of loaded potato skins, elevated by the air fryer's ability to achieve a satisfying crunch.
- ✓ Customize your toppings for a personalized and flavorful experience.

4. Stuffed Mushrooms:
- ✓ Delight in bite-sized, air-fried stuffed mushrooms with savory fillings.

✓ Explore various stuffing combinations to suit different occasions and palates.

5. Crispy Spring Rolls:
✓ Unveil the secrets to achieving a delicate and crispy exterior for homemade spring rolls.
✓ Experiment with diverse fillings, from classic vegetables to inventive flavor profiles.

CREATIVE IDEAS FOR UNIQUE AIR-FRIED STARTERS

1. Air-Fried Avocado Fries:
✓ Indulge in the creamy texture of avocado encased in a crispy, seasoned coating.
✓ Explore dipping sauces that complement the richness of the avocado.

2. Buffalo Cauliflower Bites:
✓ Transform cauliflower into spicy, tangy bites that rival traditional Buffalo wings.

✓ Learn to balance heat and flavor for a crowd-pleasing appetizer.

3. Sesame Soy Edamame:
✓ Elevate the humble edamame with a crispy exterior infused with sesame and soy flavors.
✓ Explore different seasonings and coatings to create a unique twist.

4. Caprese Skewers:
✓ Create elegant and bite-sized Caprese skewers with air-fried mozzarella bites, cherry tomatoes, and fresh basil.
✓ Experiment with drizzles of balsamic glaze for added depth.

5. Bacon-Wrapped Jalapeño Poppers:
✓ Experience the perfect combination of heat and savory goodness with air-fried bacon-wrapped jalapeño poppers.

- ✓ Explore variations, such as different cheeses and fillings, to suit your preferences.

As you delve into the world of air-fried appetizers and snacks, let your creativity flow and experiment with unique flavor combinations. Join us in the upcoming chapters of "Air Fryer Recipe Instructor" as we continue to explore the art and science of air frying, guiding you through a culinary journey filled with delicious discoveries.

CHAPTER 7
HEALTHY AIR FRYER COOKING

Welcome to a chapter dedicated to transforming your culinary experience into a healthier and more wholesome venture within "Air Fryer Recipe Instructor: The Art and Science of Air Frying." In this section, we'll explore strategic approaches for crafting healthier versions of your favorite fried foods using the air fryer. Additionally, we'll unravel the nutritional benefits that make air frying a cornerstone of a balanced and mindful culinary lifestyle.

STRATEGIES FOR CREATING HEALTHIER VERSIONS OF YOUR FAVORITE FRIED FOODS

1. **Optimal Oil Usage:**
   ✓ Discover techniques for minimizing oil while preserving the crispy texture of your dishes.

- ✓ Explore alternatives such as olive oil sprays and brushing for controlled and even distribution.

2. Healthier Coating Options:
- ✓ Explore alternative coatings such as whole-grain breadcrumbs, crushed nuts, or even air-fried panko for added fiber and nutrients.
- ✓ Learn to balance flavor and texture while reducing reliance on traditional frying batters.

3. Incorporating More Vegetables:
- ✓ Embrace the versatility of the air fryer for cooking vegetables, transforming them into crispy and flavorful snacks.
- ✓ Experiment with vegetable-based alternatives for classic fried dishes.

4. Lean Proteins:
- ✓ Opt for lean protein sources such as skinless poultry, fish, or plant-based proteins for a healthier air-fried experience.

✓ Discover marinating and seasoning strategies to enhance flavor without relying on excessive fats.

5. **Reducing Sodium Content:**
   ✓ Explore ways to reduce sodium content in your air-fried creations without compromising taste.
   ✓ Experiment with herbs, spices, and other flavor enhancers to achieve a perfect balance.

NUTRITIONAL BENEFITS OF AIR FRYING

1. **Reduced Oil Absorption:**
   ✓ Understand how air frying significantly reduces the amount of oil absorbed by ingredients compared to traditional frying.
   ✓ Explore the impact on calorie and fat content in your favorite dishes.

2. **Preservation of Nutrients:**

- ✓ Delve into the nutritional benefits of air frying, as it retains more nutrients in vegetables compared to boiling or traditional frying.
- ✓ Learn how to maximize the nutritional value of your meals through thoughtful air fryer cooking.

3. Lower Formation of Harmful Compounds:
- ✓ Explore the reduced formation of harmful compounds compared to deep frying at high temperatures.
- ✓ Understand the health implications of minimizing exposure to potentially harmful substances.

4. Healthier Heart Choices:
- ✓ Uncover how air frying aligns with heart-healthy cooking choices by minimizing the use of saturated fats.
- ✓ Discover recipes that cater to cardiovascular health without sacrificing taste.

5. Weight Management:
- ✓ Discuss how air frying can be a valuable tool in weight management by reducing overall calorie intake.
- ✓ Learn about portion control strategies and mindful eating in the context of air frying.

By incorporating these strategies and understanding the nutritional advantages, you'll embark on a journey of healthy air frying, transforming your favorite dishes into nourishing and guilt-free delights. Join us in the subsequent chapters of "Air Fryer Recipe Instructor" as we continue to explore the art and science of air frying for a wholesome culinary experience.

CHAPTER 8
MAIN COURSE MASTERY

Welcome to the heart of your air frying culinary journey within "Air Fryer Recipe Instructor: The Art and Science of Air Frying." In this chapter, we dive into the realm of main courses, where succulence meets the perfect balance of crispiness and juiciness. Join us as we explore an array of mouthwatering recipes for air-fried meats, poultry, and seafood, accompanied by techniques that will elevate your main course creations to culinary excellence.

RECIPES FOR SUCCULENT AIR-FRIED MEATS, POULTRY, AND SEAFOOD

1. **Perfectly Grilled Steaks:**
   ✓ Explore the art of air-frying steaks to achieve a beautifully seared exterior and a juicy, flavorful center.

- ✓ Learn to customize cooking times based on thickness and desired doneness.

2. Crispy Skinned Salmon:
- ✓ Delight in the texture contrast of a crispy skin enveloping perfectly cooked salmon.
- ✓ Experiment with different marinades and seasonings to enhance the natural flavors.

3. Golden-Brown Breaded Chicken Cutlets:
- ✓ Master the technique of achieving a golden-brown, crispy coating on air-fried chicken cutlets.
- ✓ Discover variations in breading and seasoning for diverse flavor profiles.

4. Juicy Air-Fried Pork Chops:
- ✓ Unlock the secrets to retaining moisture in air-fried pork chops while achieving a delectably crispy crust.

- ✓ Explore marinades and rubs to infuse rich flavors into every bite.

5. Tender and Crispy Air-Fried Shrimp:
- ✓ Revel in the succulence of perfectly air-fried shrimp, balancing tenderness with a delightful crunch.
- ✓ Experiment with different coatings and dipping sauces for a personalized touch.

TECHNIQUES FOR ACHIEVING THE PERFECT BALANCE OF CRISPINESS AND JUICINESS

1. Pre-Heating for Searing:
- ✓ Understand the significance of pre-heating in achieving a quick sear for locking in juices.
- ✓ Explore pre-heating techniques for different proteins to optimize cooking results.

2. The Two-Temperature Method:

- ✓ Explore the two-temperature method for achieving the perfect balance—initial high temperature for crispiness followed by a lower temperature for juiciness.
- ✓ Understand how this method preserves moisture while ensuring a satisfying texture.

3. Resting Periods:
- ✓ Grasp the importance of allowing meats to rest after air frying to redistribute juices.
- ✓ Learn how resting contributes to a juicier and more flavorful end result.

4. Brining and Marinating:
- ✓ Discover the benefits of brining and marinating for enhancing flavor and moisture retention.
- ✓ Experiment with different brines and marinades to suit various proteins.

5. Using Meat Thermometers:

- ✓ Embrace the precision of using a meat thermometer to achieve the desired doneness without overcooking.
- ✓ Explore recommended internal temperatures for different meats and seafood.

As you embark on the journey of main course mastery in your air fryer, these recipes and techniques will empower you to create memorable and mouthwatering dishes. Join us in the following chapters of "Air Fryer Recipe Instructor" as we continue to unravel the art and science of air frying for a culinary experience that transcends the ordinary.

CHAPTER 9
VEGETARIAN DELIGHTS

Step into the vibrant world of vegetarian culinary excellence within "Air Fryer Recipe Instructor: The Art and Science of Air Frying." In this chapter, we'll explore the realm of mouthwatering air-fried vegetarian and vegan dishes, showcasing the incredible versatility of the air fryer. Join us as we unveil delightful recipes and offer tips for preserving the natural flavors and textures of vegetables, ensuring each bite is a celebration of plant-based goodness.

MOUTHWATERING AIR-FRIED VEGETARIAN AND VEGAN DISHES

1. **Crispy Vegetable Spring Rolls:**
   - ✓ Experience the perfect fusion of crispiness and freshness with air-fried vegetable spring rolls.

- ✓ Explore creative vegetable combinations and dipping sauces for a delightful appetizer or snack.

2. Stuffed Portobello Mushrooms:
- ✓ Elevate the humble portobello mushroom to a savory and satisfying main course.
- ✓ Experiment with diverse fillings, from grains to vegetables, to create a hearty and wholesome dish.

3. Air-Fried Falafel:
- ✓ Delight in the golden-brown exterior and flavorful interior of air-fried falafel.
- ✓ Explore variations in herbs and spices for a personalized touch.

4. Vegan Buffalo Cauliflower Bites:
- ✓ Transform cauliflower into spicy, tangy bites that rival their meat counterparts.

- ✓ Experiment with different buffalo sauces and vegan dipping options.

5. **Sweet Potato Fries with Avocado Dip:**
   - ✓ Indulge in the perfect balance of sweetness and crispiness with air-fried sweet potato fries.
   - ✓ Pair them with a creamy avocado dip for a satisfying and nutritious snack.

TIPS FOR PRESERVING THE NATURAL FLAVORS AND TEXTURES OF VEGETABLES

1. **Proper Cutting Techniques:**
   - ✓ Learn the importance of uniform cutting for even cooking and preserving the natural textures of vegetables.
   - ✓ Experiment with different cuts, such as julienne or cubed, for diverse results.

2. **Minimal Oil Usage:**

- ✓ Discover techniques for achieving crispiness with minimal oil, allowing the inherent flavors of vegetables to shine.
- ✓ Experiment with different oil alternatives for a health-conscious approach.

3. **Layering for Even Cooking:**
   - ✓ Understand the significance of proper layering to ensure even air circulation around vegetables.
   - ✓ Learn how to avoid overcrowding for optimal results.

4. **Seasoning Enhancements:**
   - ✓ Explore seasoning blends that complement and enhance the natural flavors of vegetables.
   - ✓ Experiment with fresh herbs, citrus, and spices to elevate the taste profile.

5. **Creative Marinades:**

- ✓ Unlock the potential of creative marinades for infusing vegetables with robust flavors.
- ✓ Discover marinade combinations that add depth without overshadowing the inherent qualities of the ingredients.

As you explore the vegetarian delights achievable with your air fryer, let your creativity flourish and savor the vibrant flavors of plant-based cuisine. Join us in the subsequent chapters of "Air Fryer Recipe Instructor" as we continue to unravel the art and science of air frying, providing inspiration for every culinary preference.

CHAPTER 10

SWEETS AND TREATS

Indulge your sweet tooth and explore the sweet side of air frying in this delightful chapter of "Air Fryer Recipe Instructor: The Art and Science of Air Frying." Here, we'll delve into the realm of delectable desserts and sweet treats crafted with the precision and efficiency of your air fryer. Join us as we uncover the versatility of this kitchen marvel beyond savory dishes, elevating your culinary repertoire to new heights.

DELECTABLE DESSERTS AND SWEET TREATS MADE IN THE AIR FRYER

1. **Air-Fried Apple Fritters:**
   - ✓ Experience the joy of warm, cinnamon-spiced apple fritters with a golden-brown exterior.
   - ✓ Learn techniques for achieving a fluffy interior that contrasts beautifully with the crispy coating.

2. Chocolate Molten Lava Cakes:
- ✓ Delight in the decadence of individual chocolate molten lava cakes with gooey, luscious centers.
- ✓ Explore variations in cocoa intensity and experiment with different fillings.

3. Cinnamon Sugar Donut Holes:
- ✓ Embrace the nostalgia of bite-sized donut holes, perfectly air-fried to a golden perfection.
- ✓ Customize coatings and dipping sauces for a playful dessert experience.

4. Blueberry Lemon Scones:
- ✓ Elevate your tea time with light and flaky blueberry lemon scones, each with a golden-brown exterior.
- ✓ Discover tips for incorporating fruit into baked goods for a burst of freshness.

5. **Air-Fried Churros with Chocolate Dipping Sauce:**
   ✓ Transport yourself to a carnival with air-fried churros, dusted in cinnamon sugar and paired with a rich chocolate dipping sauce.
   ✓ Master the art of achieving a crispy exterior and a soft, airy interior.

EXPLORING THE VERSATILITY OF THE AIR FRYER BEYOND SAVORY DISHES

1. **Quick and Crispy Fruit Chips:**
   ✓ Transform your favorite fruits into crispy and addictive chips using the air fryer.
   ✓ Explore a variety of fruits and seasoning options for a healthy and satisfying snack.

2. **Maple Glazed Nuts:**
   ✓ Elevate your nut game with air-fried maple-glazed nuts—perfect for snacking or as a topping for desserts and salads.

- ✓ Understand the nuances of achieving a glossy and flavorful glaze.

3. Puff Pastry Delights:
- ✓ Unleash the versatility of puff pastry in the air fryer, creating flaky and delightful pastries.
- ✓ Explore sweet fillings like fruits, chocolate, and nuts for a sophisticated treat.

4. Homemade Beignets:
- ✓ Bring a touch of New Orleans to your kitchen with homemade beignets, light and pillowy, and perfectly air-fried.
- ✓ Experiment with powdered sugar, glazes, or fruit compotes for a personalized touch.

5. Stuffed French Toast Bites:
- ✓ Elevate breakfast or brunch with air-fried stuffed French toast bites, oozing with sweet fillings.

- ✓ Explore variations in fillings, from cream cheese to fruit preserves.

As you explore the sweet possibilities of your air fryer, you'll discover a world of indulgence and creativity that extends far beyond savory dishes. Join us in the following chapters of "Air Fryer Recipe Instructor" as we continue to unravel the art and science of air frying for a culinary experience that encompasses the full spectrum of flavors and occasions.

Printed in Great Britain
by Amazon